MEDITERRANEAN DIET

A Quick and Easy Guide to Creating Nutrient Rich, Heart Healthy Dishes in 30 Minutes or Less

Includes 7-Day Quick Start Meal Plan

STELLA ROMANO

MEDITERRANEAN DIET

GET YOUR 3 BONUSES HERE

www.empirepublishingso.wixsite.com/mediterranean-diet-1

TABLE OF CONTENTS

INTRODUCTION

"The doctor of the future will no longer treat the human frame with drugs but rather will cure and prevent disease with nutrition."

– Thomas Edison.

F ed up with feeling tired? Lacking energy? Desperate to lose weight, but nothing seems to work? The Mediterranean Diet is one of the best diets for overall health and wellness. The diet boasts incredible healing powers based primarily on vegetables, fruits, legumes, and healthy fats, with only small amounts of meat and dairy consumed. It goes a long way toward explaining why Mediterranean people live longer, healthier lives than many other people worldwide.

This book is designed to help you understand the Mediterranean diet, how it works, and how it benefits your health in so many ways. Most people who follow the diet do so because they have high blood pressure, heart disease, or another chronic condition, and their doctor has recommended the Mediterranean Diet to help their symptoms.

There is no one-size-fits-all approach to this diet. There is no specific Mediterranean Diet, and that's because the different countries on the Med all follow slightly different diets based on what foods are available. However, the Harvard School of Public Health got together with the World Health Organization's European office and Oldways Preservation and Exchange Trust in 1993 and jointly produced what is known as the Mediterranean Diet Pyramid. Rather than a prescribed diet, this was a guideline to help people understand the best foods to eat based on the diet followed by people who lived in Southern Italy, Crete, and Southern Spain in the middle of the 20th century. That's because those countries had the lowest instances of chronic disease and tended to live longer lives, even though healthcare wasn't the best at that time. The main explanation for this was their diet – fresh fruit and vegetables, nuts, beans, whole grains, olive oil, red wine, fish, and a little dairy. However, it is also due to exercise and the fact that these people eat their meals together, as a family, and make it an enjoyable, social event – every meal.

When you read this book, do it with an open mind. Don't pick it up because it's touted as the best way to lose weight. Pick it up and read it because you want to lead a healthier, happier, longer life and because you want to feel well with plenty of energy.

How This Book Will Help You

This book will teach you everything you need to know about the Mediterranean diet and how it will improve your life.

- **Chapter 1:** This chapter provides a brief overview of the diet, its health benefits, key principles, and a look at where it all began. You'll learn why you should adopt this lifestyle, how to embrace it wholeheartedly, and a look at how to use the best ingredients to create delicious, healthy meals.

- **Chapter 2:** This chapter discusses the health benefits the diet provides and how to incorporate healthy Mediterranean habits into your lifestyle. You'll also learn why you should include certain herbs, spices, and foods to provide incredible flavor and texture.

- **Chapter 3:** Here's where you will learn about the crucial ingredients you need to create amazing Mediterranean meals and some tips on the Mediterranean practice of mindful eating.

- **Chapters 4, 5, 6, 7, 8, and 9:** These chapters are dedicated to bringing you some of the best breakfast, lunch, dinner, dessert, and snack recipes, along with nutritional information and tips on incorporating certain ingredients.

- **Chapter 10:** This chapter provides you with a 7-day meal planner and sample grocery list.

- **Chapter 11:** This chapter discusses seasonings and how to use them to create amazing flavors.

- **Chapter 12:** This chapter looks at how to follow the Mediterranean Diet on a budget, including plenty of useful tips.

This book is a stepping stone, your first stop on a journey to health, wellness, and a happy life, so head to Chapter 1 and take that first step to a new you.

CHAPTER 1

INTRODUCTION TO THE MEDITERRANEAN DIET

The Mediterranean Diet is touted as one of the most healthy and there are plenty of good reasons for that. It has been shown to reduce the risk of many chronic conditions and diseases, such as heart disease, some cancers, metabolic syndrome, depression, and diabetes, and it has also been shown to improve mental and physical functioning in older people. This chapter will talk you through the Mediterranean Diet and everything you need to know about getting started.

What Is the Mediterranean Diet?

The Mediterranean Diet isn't actually a diet. It is a way of eating, a lifestyle pattern that follows the traditional eating patterns of Mediterranean countries. But you don't need to live in the Med to follow it and, these days, more and more people are adopting it to benefit from its health benefits.

It is not a strict eating plan. Each country in the Mediterranean follows a slightly different diet based on what foods are locally available. It is largely plant-based, with plenty of fruits, vegetables, legumes, whole grains, and healthy olive oil. Fish is allowed, indeed recommended over pork, red meat, and poultry, although you can eat some lean poultry. Eggs and dairy foods are allowed, so long as they are consumed in moderation, while processed foods are significantly limited.

The Mediterranean Diet has been linked with lower risks of strokes, heart disease, Alzheimer's, and Parkinson's, and it can also lower cholesterol levels and help you live a longer life. New research has also shown that it can benefit people with some cancers, diabetes type 2, anxiety, and depression.

Mediterranean Diet Guidelines

Unlike many other diets you have no doubt tried, the Mediterranean Diet is not restrictive. However, because it varies from country to country and even between regions in each country, there are some guidelines you can follow to help you understand the diet.

The Mediterranean Diet Pyramid was created in 1993 by Oldways, the WHO, and the Harvard School of Public Health in a bid to provide people with a healthy alternative to the food pyramid created by the USDA.

If you struggle to know what to eat, a simple rule is this: half your plate should be veggies and fruits, a quarter should be healthy protein, and a quarter should be whole grains. Rather than focusing on specific foods, the diet is more based on food groups, which makes it much easier to tailor it to different flavors, cuisine types, and food intolerances or lifestyle choices.

Here's what you need to know:

- **The Focus Is on Whole Foods:** Processed foods are rarely eaten on the Mediterranean diet, so if it is in a packet, look at the label. Opt for foods with whole-food ingredients, like nuts, whole grains, or legumes, and avoid those with added ingredients. Your focus should be on fruits, veggies, healthy oils, and fish.

- **Veggies and Fruits Are the Largest Part of Your Meals:** When you follow the Mediterranean Diet, you should consume at least seven to ten servings of these every day, although as little as three to five will also benefit your cardiovascular system. Add more veggies to your meals – have some spinach with eggs, add cucumber and avocado to your sandwich, and, instead of an unhealthy snack, have apple slices spread with peanut butter, berries in yogurt, a handful of mixed raw nuts, or dried fruit with oatmeal.

- **Eat More Fish:** The main protein sources on the Mediterranean Diet are salmon, tuna, mackerel, and other fatty fish. These provide good levels of omega-3 fatty acids, which help lower cholesterol and inflammation levels. If you can't get fresh, use canned fish, as they offer just as much nutrition, are much easier to prepare, and have a long shelf-life. Shellfish and white fish also provide a good source of lean protein but don't have as much omega-3. You can also eat other lean sources of animal protein.

- **Use Plant-Based Oils for Cooking:** Plant-based oils are much healthier and are the main source of fat in the Mediterranean Diet. Some people balk at eating fat, believing it is bad, but not all fats are equal. The Mediterranean Diet doesn't limit the amount of fat you can eat. Instead, it focuses on getting it from healthy sources, like olive oil, which is good for the heart. You can also use sesame, peanut, avocado, canola, and sunflower oil.

- **Moderate Your Dairy Intake:** Rather than eating heavy cream and full-fat cheese with every meal, focus on eating different cheese varieties and other dairy products but in moderation. Fermented dairy products like yogurt are particularly good, as are Parmesan, feta, and other strong cheeses, where you only need a small amount. Limit how much processed cheese you eat. In terms of yogurt, choose plain Greek yogurt where you can and avoid eating high-sugar yogurts with added flavor.

- **Choose Whole Grains Over Refined:** Swap white bread, pasta, and rice for whole grains, like farro, brown rice, barley, quinoa, whole grain bread, and corn. Whole grains are a big part of the diet and can help keep your blood sugar stable, lower cholesterol, and help you maintain a healthy weight. They are also excellent sources of fiber and B vitamins. Legumes and beans are also a big part of the diet and have similar benefits.

- **Choose Nuts to Snack on:** Nuts may be high in fat, but it is heart-healthy fat. They also contain fiber and protein, and all of these are excellent for longer satiety and lower inflammation and cholesterol. If you want snacks between meals, try a quarter cup of nuts, especially walnuts, which are higher in omega-3.

- **Ditch Added Sugars:** When you eat processed foods, you eat a higher amount of added sugar, which isn't a regular part of the Mediterranean Diet. While you don't have to ditch them altogether, stick to eating small amounts on rare occasions, just as a treat. On the whole, you should eat fruit when you crave sugar.

- **Drink Moderate Amounts of Red Wine:** You can safely consume a glass of red wine per day (two for men) with a meal. However, if you don't normally drink alcohol, don't add it in just because you can.

While this will be discussed later, the foods you should try to avoid or limit:

- Processed foods, including baked goods and processed meat products.
- Red meat.
- Added sugars and other refined carbs.
- Beer and liquor.
- Sweetened drinks.

Where Did the Mediterranean Diet Originate?

Contrary to popular belief, the Mediterranean Diet is not a diet but a lifestyle and isn't tied to one country. Every region has its own version of the diet, depending on the availability of local foods. Where they are the same is that all versions of the diet are based heavily on vegetables, fruits, and olive oil.

In 1945, Dr. Ancel Keys was based in Salerno, Italy, and that's where he first studied the diet. However, it wasn't until 1958 that his work was given attention, and that's when he started what became known as the Seven Countries Study. The study looked at the links between diet and lifestyle and health conditions, such as heart disease and strokes, in seven countries across four regions – Japan, the USA, Northern Europe, and Southern Europe. The study encompassed more than 12,000 male participants.

The results showed that Northern Europe and the USA had much higher levels of deaths from strokes and heart disease than Japan and Southern Europe. More research was conducted, and this showed that each region differed significantly in their diets and lifestyles, and this data is a big part of what makes the Mediterranean Diet so popular today. More studies were published in the 1990s, all showing the same results, and this has led to the Mediterranean Diet becoming more widely adopted in the Western world.

Incorporating Seasonal Goods

The Mediterranean Diet focuses on whole foods, and while you can buy these from any grocery store, there is a big emphasis on eating seasonal foods. But what does this mean? Every season brings a new variety of fresh fruits, veggies, nuts, and seeds, each growing in different conditions. For example, apples are perfect in the colder months of fall and winter, while beetroot, tomatoes, cucumbers, and other salad veggies grow well in the heat of spring and summer.

The Benefits of Seasonal Foods

1. They are much healthier.

Seasonal fruits and vegetables are healthier than anything you buy in a grocery store. They taste far better and are packed with nutrients because they are picked at their peak ripeness. Much of what you buy out of season, and sometimes in season in a grocery store, has been treated with pesticides, chemical fertilizers, wax, and some preservatives. There are two reasons for this: out-of-season foods are preserved to ensure they last longer, and they often travel hundreds or thousands of miles to get to the store. Buying from a local store or farmer's market, or even growing your own, is far better – the quicker they get onto your plate, the healthier they are for you.

- **You get the widest variety of produce.**

Every season brings new vegetables and fruits, so you always have a great selection of fresh produce to choose from. That means you never get bored because you won't always eat the same things and get the best range of minerals, vitamins, and nutrients.

- **It's cheaper.**

Buying in season is always cheaper. When the harvests come in, there is always a glut of produce, which means it can be sold at cheaper prices. When you buy locally, you know that the produce won't have to be stored and then be transported across the country or from somewhere else in the world, which also keeps the cost down.

- **It benefits the environment.**

Because seasonal produce is grown naturally, you know it hasn't been sprayed with chemicals that leach into the soil and run into the ecosystem or water supply. Many organic farmers grow under nets to keep pests away, use interplanting and companion planting to benefit the crops and act as pest deterrents, and weed by hand. Seasonal eating also reduces the CO_2 released, as the crops don't require anywhere near as much energy to grow them and don't need to be transported. The shorter the distance it has to travel, the better the environmental benefits.

- **You support your local economy.**

Buying seasonal produce from local suppliers means you support them and their bid to farm sustainably. Smaller farms tend to be labor-intensive, and grocery stores don't pay much for their produce. If they can sell it locally, everyone wins – you get fresh, nutrient-rich food, they get more of the profits, and the whole community benefits.

Customizing the Mediterranean Diet

Because the Mediterranean Diet is mostly plant-based, it is easy to customize it for your dietary requirements or lifestyle choices.

Here are the food swaps you can make to customize it for you:

Vegetarian/Vegan:

- Switch meat and fish for chickpeas, lentils, black beans, and other legumes in your burgers, stews, and salads.
- Switch meat and fish for edamame, tempeh, seitan, or tofu in sandwiches and stir-fries. Silken tofu goes well in mousses, quiches, or other creamy dishes.
- Mix chia or flaxseed with water to make a vegan egg replacement.

Lactose Intolerant:

- Switch cow's milk for coconut, soy, almond, oat, or other plant-based milk in your drinks and cooking.
- Choose yogurts made from soy, almond, or coconut milk, but do watch the sugar content.
- Choose vegan cheeses made from coconut, soy, or nut milk.

Gluten Intolerance:

- Switch wheat for quinoa and rice, barley for amaranth and millet, and rye for corn and buckwheat. This includes any product that may include those ingredients, such as bread, flour, etc.

Healthy Fats:

- Ditch the mayo or butter and use mashed avocado as a spread on sandwiches or toast.
- Switch vegetable and animal fats with olive oil for cooking, salad dressings, and drizzling.

CHAPTER 2

THE BENEFITS OF THE MEDITERRANEAN DIET

There is plenty of evidence to suggest that the Mediterranean Diet offers plenty of health benefits, not least reducing the risks of chronic disease and early death in women and men. It has been voted the healthiest diet of the year for the last several years running, and here's why:

- **It helps Reduce Type 2 Diabetes and Obesity:** Both lead to a much higher risk of stroke and heart disease, among other issues. Five separate studies have shown that obese people following the Mediterranean Diet lost more weight than those on other diets, like low-fat and low-carb diets.

- **It Reduces the Risk of Heart Disease and Stroke in Women:** A long-term Nurses Study was designed to study nurses and identify chronic illness risk factors. A 20-year follow-upshowed that women who followed the Mediterranean diet and stuck to it were at a much lower risk of stroke and heart disease than those who didn't.

- **It Improves Your Gut Health:** A European study examined how those who stayed on the Mediterranean Diet for at least a year had much better gut health, lowering the risk of early aging, poor cognition, and frailty.

- **It Reduces the Risks of Cognitive Decline and Dementia:** Long-term studies have shown that people who follow the Mediterranean Diet permanently have a lower risk of cognitive decline and dementia.

- **It Can Reduce the Risk of Some Cancers:** The Mediterranean Diet has been shown to improve the risk factors for prostate, breast, and colorectal cancers, three of the most common worldwide.

- **It Can Lower High Blood Pressure:** High blood pressure can lead to strokes and heart disease, but the healthy Mediterranean Diet has been shown to help reduce blood pressure and reduce the risks.

- **It Can Help with Weight Loss:** Some evidence shows that following the Mediterranean Diet can help you lose weight, but you must pair it with exercise o or activity of some description to get the best results. It can also help you maintain a healthy weight.

The Mediterranean Diet and Inflammation

What is inflammation? Have you ever cut your finger, and it gets all swollen and red? Knocked your knee, and that swells up? That's inflammation, but what does it do to you inside?

Slight inflammation is actually good for your body as it can help the healing process. But when it turns to chronic inflammation, it raises the risk factors for disease. It can damage your brain, heart, and other organs and is the underlying factor for virtually all major illnesses, including depression, heart disease, some cancers, and Alzheimer's Disease.

In the same way that injury can cause inflammation, so too can some health conditions, and even some foods you eat. Conversely, some foods you should eat (and some you should cut out) help soothe inflammation and even prevent it from occurring in the first place.

Because we have different triggers, there are a number of reasons why you might suffer from inflammation in your body. The main factor is chronic illness. If you have a chronic condition, it could be caused by chronic inflammation. Some of those conditions include:

- Crohn's disease.
- Heart disease.
- Hypertension.
- Irritable bowel syndrome.
- Multiple sclerosis.
- Obesity.
- Psoriasis.

- Rheumatoid arthritis.
- Type 1 diabetes.
- Ulcerative colitis.

The Mediterranean Diet is based on some of the world's best anti-inflammatory ingredients, including fruit, veggies, lean protein, whole grains, spices, herbs, and some of the healthiest fat sources – olive oil, chia seeds, avocado, walnuts, etc. These foods are packed with antioxidants, minerals, and vitamins to keep inflammation at bay and boost your immune system.

The Mediterranean Mindset

The Mediterranean Diet is about more than just food. It is a lifestyle, not a diet, which means you should adopt the Mediterranean mindset if you want to switch to a healthy diet for life. Recently, a study from Harvard on the Mediterranean lifestyle concluded that plenty of rest, socialization, and physical activity were key points in lowering the risk of heart disease and increasing longevity.

Adopting that mindset means incorporating the following habits into your daily life:

1. Living an Active Life

The biggest risk factor for chronic disease and early death is living a sedentary lifestyle. That's why physical activity is one of the biggest factors in the Mediterranean lifestyle. This doesn't mean you have to go to the gym every day. You can go for a walk, bike ride, swim, or even do some gardening. Get together with your friends for a weekend game of friendly tennis, head to the park for a kick around with a ball, anything that gets you moving and that, just as importantly, you enjoy doing.

Plenty of research shows that physical activity and the Mediterranean Diet are mutually beneficial. Following the diet has the same benefits as walking around 4000 extra steps per day, while the diet itself gives you the energy to take up some form of exercise and stick to it.

2. Socialization

If you visit any Mediterranean country, one thing will stand out – the strong culture of socialization. Friends and family are a priority, and nearly every meal is a social occasion. Many shops close for a few hours in the afternoon for a social lunch, allowing people to take their time over their meals and catch up with everyone. Socialization has long been linked to better mental health and happiness, leading to a happier and longer life.

3. Practicing Mindful Eating

Following a Mediterranean lifestyle means being aware of how you eat, perhaps more so than what you eat. Some of their practices include cutting portion sizes by using smaller plates, changing their cooking methods (i.e., ditching frying for baking), and eating slowly. This leads to improvements in digestion, which benefits the gut.

4. Getting the Work-Life Balance Right

A balanced life is central to Mediterranean culture, which means work does not overtake everything else in life, leaving time for relaxation and rest. When you take time for yourself and get involved in things that interest you, your stress levels are reduced, and you feel much better overall, so getting the work-life balance right is critical to health and well-being.

5.   Using Olive Oil Generously

Olive oil is one of the most-consumed sources of healthy fat in the Mediterranean and has long been shown to help increase lifespan and lower chronic disease risk factors. Olive oil is high in monounsaturated fats and contains generous amounts of antioxidants, particularly polyphenols. This antioxidant has been shown to have incredible health benefits, including weight loss, lower LDL cholesterol, higher HDL cholesterol, stable blood sugar levels, and lower blood pressure. It also provides the hair and skin with a good, healthy glow. However, you shouldn't use any olive oil. It should be the highest quality, extra virgin olive oil, which is the purest and offers the most health benefits.

6.   Getting Enough Rest

When you go on holiday to the Med, you may have noticed that many people settle down in the afternoons for a siesta. This is because siestas allow the body to rest and rejuvenate, which leads to lower stress levels and better cognitive functioning. It has recently been shown in a Harvard study that siestas are as important as socialization and physical activity in increasing life span and lowering the risks of heart disease, among other chronic conditions.

7.   Eating Local and Seasonal Foods

The Mediterranean Diet is based mostly on whole foods, healthy fat, and lean protein, so it's no surprise that most of that should come from seasonal, local foods. This doesn't just support local farmers and businesses. It also provides you with the most nutrients in every fruit or veggie you eat, and it cuts your carbon footprint significantly.

8. Learn to Embrace Nature

Cultures right across the Mediterranean are deeply connected to nature. When you spend time in nature, your mental health benefits, your stress levels are reduced, and you learn to love the natural environment.

9. Focus on Mental Health and Happiness

Embracing the Mediterranean lifestyle means getting involved in activities that you enjoy, socializing with friends and family, and learning to have a positive outlook, all of which improve mental health. This leads to more happiness and a longer life.

Getting Started on the Mediterranean Diet

Changing how you eat is a big thing. If your body is used to being fed fried, processed, or junk food, it may not like it when you suddenly change your diet and start feeding it all that nutritious, healthy food. Everyone can follow this lifestyle, regardless of what they are used to, but you don't have to go all in right at the start. Some simple food swaps will have you well on the way, and it won't take long for you to transition to a full Mediterranean diet.

1. Use Olive Oil Instead of Seed and Vegetable Oils

Vegetable and seed oils might seem healthy because they don't have any saturated fat in them, and they have high levels of omega-6 fatty acids. While your body requires these fatty acids, the average diet contains far too many of them and nowhere near enough omega-3. Most processed foods are made with vegetable oils, which are considered inflammatory and strongly associated with diabetes, obesity, and metabolic syndrome. However, perhaps more importantly, seed and vegetable oils lack the antioxidants found in abundance in olive oil.

2.   Use Tomato Sauce on Veggies Instead of Melted Cheese or Butter

Many people don't really like vegetables but know they need to eat more. While this is good, all the health benefits are eliminated when you top them with butter or melted cheese to make them taste better. Instead of butter and cheese, use herbs and tomato sauce on your veggies, just the way they do in the Med. This lowers the amount of saturated fat you consume and increases your veggie intake – the tomatoes in the sauce.

3.   Eat Chicken or Fish Instead of Red Meat

More and more research shows that red meat can raise your risks of diabetes, some cancers, and heart disease. While the Mediterranean Diet is mainly plant-based, some meat can be eaten. This should be lean, organic chicken or fish, both versatile and can be cooked in many different ways.

4.   Top Baked Potatoes with Greek Yogurt and Olive Oil Instead of Sour Cream and Butter

Baked potatoes may taste delicious, topped with sour cream and butter, but Greek yogurt and olive oil are just as nice and healthier. Making this swap turns an unhealthy meal into one loaded with antioxidants and healthy fats.

5. Use Olive Oil and Vinegar-Based Dressings Instead of Creamy Ones

Creamy dressings are typically made from cheese, mayonnaise, and other unhealthy ingredients. Use vinegar and olive oil as your base, and add other healthy ingredients, like mustard or honey, depending on your salad. The olive oil provides the healthy fats, and you only need a little of it for maximum antioxidant absorption. When you consume a dressing filled with polyunsaturated and saturated fats, you need a lot more of it for your body to absorb the antioxidants.

6. Have Plain Greek Yogurt Instead of Flavored Yogurt

Yes, it may contain fruit, but it isn't raw fruit, and flavored yogurt also contains tons of sugar or sweeteners, not to mention preservatives, gelatin, and thickeners. Sheep's milk yogurt is far more nutritious than cow's milk, but if you can't get it, look for plain Greek yogurt.

Other steps you can take are:

- Swapping refined grains with legumes and whole grains.
- Drinking water instead of sugary beverages – you can always add slices of lemon, lime, cucumber, or any other fruit or veg to give it flavor and get an extra dose of minerals and vitamins.
- Have at least one vegetarian or vegan meal per week.

Try these steps to help you transition:

- If you have eggs for breakfast, add some spinach.
- Instead of cookies or candy, have slices of apple spread with nut butter for a snack.
- When you go out to eat, ditch the steak and order salmon instead.
- Use a little olive oil instead of butter or vegetable oil to sauté your vegetables.

Little steps add up to big changes, and you will reap the benefits in time.

In the next chapter, you will discover all the delicious ingredients you can eat and those you should eliminate or at least cut back on significantly.

CHAPTER 3

ESSENTIAL INGREDIENTS

Starting a new diet is not always easy, but the first step is to know what you can and cannot eat. Most diets are highly restrictive, which is why people never stick to them. The Mediterranean Diet is more of a lifestyle and is nowhere near as restrictive. In many ways, because the diet differs between countries, defining food lists is not easy.

However, keep in mind that the Mediterranean Diet is:

- Mostly plant-based.
- Low in meat and animal products.
- Includes seafood or fish twice a week at least.

Food and Beverages to Include

While seasonal, fresh foods are preferable, you can eat dried, frozen, and canned, too, but make sure you read the labels – they shouldn't have any added ingredients, especially sodium and sugar.

Base your diet on the following:

Vegetables:

- Broccoli
- Brussels sprouts
- Cucumber
- Kale
- Onions
- Potatoes
- Spinach
- Sweet potatoes
- Tomatoes
- Turnips

Fruits:

- Apples
- Bananas
- Dates
- Figs
- Grapes
- Melons
- Oranges

- Peaches
- Pears
- Strawberries

Seeds, Nuts, Nut Butters:

- Almond butter
- Almonds
- Cashews
- Hazelnuts
- Macadamia nuts
- Peanut butter
- Pumpkin seeds
- Sunflower seeds
- Walnuts

Legumes:

- Beans
- Chickpeas
- Lentils
- Peanuts
- Peas
- Pulses

Whole Grains:

- Barley
- Brown rice
- Buckwheat

- Corn
- Oats
- Rye
- Wholewheat bread
- Wholewheat pasta

Fish and Seafood:

- Clams
- Crabs
- Mackerel
- Mussels
- Oysters
- Salmon
- Sardines
- Shrimp
- Trout
- Tuna

Lean Poultry:

- Chicken
- Duck
- Turkey

Eggs:

- Chicken
- Duck
- Quail

Dairy:

- Cheese
- Milk
- Yogurt

Herbs and Spices:

- Basil
- Cinnamon
- Garlic
- Mint
- Nutmeg
- pepper
- Rosemary
- Sage

Healthy Fats:

- Avocado
- Avocado oil
- Extra virgin olive oil
- Olives

Beverages:

- Natural fruit juices with no added sugar
- Red wine in moderation and only with a meal
- Tea and coffee, but go light on the cream and sugar
- Water

Foods to Limit

While there are no real restrictions, you should try to eliminate or at least restrict your consumption of the following foods:

Added Sugars:

This is found in a lot of different foods, but more so in the following:

- Baked goods
- Candy
- Cookies
- Ice cream
- Soda
- Syrups
- Table sugar

Refined Grains:

- Chips
- Crackers
- Pasta
- Tortillas
- White bread

Trans Fats:

Found in:

- Fried foods
- Margarine
- Processed foods

Highly Processed Foods:

- Convenience foods
- Fast foods
- Granola bars
- Microwave popcorn
- Ready meals

Beverages:

- Beer
- Liquor
- Soda and other sweetened drinks
- Sweetened fruit juices

Mediterranean Diet Characteristics

One of the biggest characteristics of the Mediterranean Diet is the fact that it is based on seasonal, locally available foods, which is why the foods change from one country to the next. It's one of the easiest diets to adapt to any lifestyle choice or dietary requirements and is even an easy diet for those who lead busy lives.

The foods you should include with virtually every meal are:

Grains

Choose whole grains because they are high in minerals, vitamins, fiber, and plenty of other nutrients. They can help you keep your cholesterol levels under control, along with blood pressure and weight, and can also help reduce the risks of conditions like heart disease and diabetes.

According to the American Dietary Guidelines, you should ensure that whole grains make up at least half of your total consumption – on the Mediterranean Diet, that should be virtually 100%.

Whole grains contain bran, which is an excellent source of fiber, and they may also contain the following nutrients – be aware that nutrient content varies between grains:

- Folate – vitamin B9
- Iron
- Magnesium
- Niacin – vitamin B3
- Phosphorus
- Pyridoxine – vitamin B6
- Riboflavin – vitamin B2
- Selenium
- Thiamin – vitamin B1
- Vitamin A
- Vitamin E

The Benefits:

Whole grains contain minerals and vitamins that benefit your health and well-being, and the fiber content can help:

- Balance good and bad cholesterol
- Lower blood pressure
- Lower insulin
- Increase satiety so you don't overeat

Eating enough fiber can help reduce the risk of type 2 diabetes, colorectal cancer, stroke, and diseases of the blood vessels and heart.

Olive Oil and Olives

These are a pivotal ingredient in any version of the Mediterranean Diet. Traditionally, olives are consumed whole, while olive oil is used to flavor and cook food. It is the main source of healthy fat and should comprise around 18 to 25% of your total fat calories. In terms of flavoring, olive oil is used to dress salads, legumes, and vegetables, and its delicious flavor tends to lead to more of these being consumed. It is also used in Mediterranean desserts, as you will find in a later chapter. Extra virgin olive oil is recommended because of its higher level of nutrients. It contains vitamin E and phenols, both rich antioxidant sources.

Fruit and Vegetables

Fruits and vegetables are the biggest part of the Mediterranean Diet, as they are packed with minerals and vitamins, most of which are antioxidants, that benefit your overall health and well-being, reducing the risk of disease. Those minerals and vitamins are:

- Beta-carotene – vitamin A
- Folic acid
- Magnesium
- Phosphorus
- Vitamin C
- Vitamin E
- Zinc

Folic acid has been shown to help reduce homocysteine levels in the blood, reducing the risk of heart disease. It has also been shown that eating fresh fruits and vegetables is far healthier for you than taking the minerals and vitamins in supplement form.

Vegetables and fruits are all low fat, low salt, and low sugar – added sugar, as they are packed with natural sugars. All fruits and veggies contain fiber and are among the best sources of it. Eating plenty of them helps you feel for longer, stopping you from overeating and feeling hungry again an hour later. Eating a good amount of fruits and vegetables can help:

- Weight loss and weight maintenance
- Lower blood pressure
- Lower cholesterol

They can also help protect you against diseases because they contain phytochemicals and antioxidants. Eating a lot of vegetables and fruits regularly can help protect you from:

- Stroke
- Type 2 diabetes
- Heart disease
- Cancer – especially throat, stomach, and bowel
- Hypertension

What Fruit You Should Eat:

You should eat fruits raw to get the best nutrients, although some can be cooked. These are the commonest fruits to include on the det:

- Apples
- Apricots
- Avocado
- Blueberries
- Grapefruits
- Honeydew melons
- Kiwis
- Lemons
- Limes
- Mandarins
- Nectarines
- Oranges
- Passionfruit
- Pears
- Peaches
- Plums
- Raspberries
- Rock melons
- Strawberries
- Tomatoes – yes, they are a fruit!
- Watermelons

What Vegetables You Should Eat:

- Asparagus
- Broccoli
- Brussel's sprouts
- Cabbage

- Cauliflower
- Celery
- Chard
- Cucumber
- Garlic
- Kale
- Lettuce
- Onion
- Potato
- Pumpkin
- Shallot
- Silverbeet
- Spinach
- Squash
- Sweet potato
- Yam
- Zucchini

What Legumes You Should Eat:

Pulses and legumes are packed with valuable nutrients but should be cooked rather than eaten raw, as this increases their nutritional qualities, helps you digest them better, and removes all harmful toxins:

- Tofu
- Soybeans
- Chickpea flour
- Lentil flour

- Soy flour
- Haricot beans
- Chickpeas
- Lentils
- Red kidney beans
- Green peas
- Green beans
- Butter beans
- Broad beans
- Snow peas

Why Color Is Important

Fruits and vegetables of the same or similar color contain the same protective properties and colors, which is why you should "eat the rainbow." That means eating a wide variety of colors daily to ensure you get all the minerals, vitamins, and other nutrient you need. Here's a brief overview:

- **Red:** Such as watermelon and tomatoes. These have a compound called lycopene, which is thought to help fight heart disease and prostate cancer.
- **Green:** Such as kale and spinach. These have zeaxanthin and lutein, which are thought to help protect your eyes from diseases related to aging.
- **Blue and Purple:** Like eggplant and blueberries. These have anthocyanins in them, thought to help protect against some cancers.

- **White:** Such as cauliflower. These have sulforaphane in them, which is said to help protect against cancer.

Protein

The 2015-2020 Dietary Guidelines recommend 5 ½ ounces of protein daily, based on eating 2000 calories and consuming a healthy diet. Most people eat too much protein, and not enough of it is lean. The Mediterranean Diet recommends eating protein from a variety of sources, including fish, eggs, beans, seeds, and nuts, which means ditching red meat and fatty cuts. It also means changing your cooking methods from frying in vegetable oil to grilling or baking. You can use an air fryer and use olive oil if you sauté anything.

Eating large amounts of saturated fats can lead to serious health issues. You should also consider that while nuts and seeds are considered healthy and should be included in your diet, too many of them can lead to you consuming more calories than you need, leading to weight gain and associated problems.

You should also watch your portions, especially if you go out to eat. Restaurants tend to serve over-sized portions of fish and meat, usually containing more protein than you need in an entire day.

Protein Sources

Proteins come from various sources, including:

- Meat
- Poultry
- Fish

- Beans
- Peas
- Nuts
- Eggs
- Seeds
- Tofu
- Greek yogurt
- Cheese
- Milk
- Vegetables
- Whole grains

Here are some of the common protein sources you can include in the Mediterranean Diet, depending on what is available in your region:

Fin Fish:

- Catfish
- Cod
- Flounder
- Haddock
- Halibut
- Herring
- Mackerel
- Pollock
- Porgy
- Salmon
- Sea bass

- Snapper
- Swordfish
- Trout
- Tuna

Shellfish:

- Clams
- Crab
- Crayfish
- Lobster
- Mussels
- Octopus
- Scallops
- Shrimp
- Squid

Canned Fish:

- Anchovies
- Clams
- Sardines
- Tuna

Poultry:

- Ground chicken
- Ground turkey
- Lean chicken breast
- Lean duck

- Lean goose
- Lean turkey breast

Eggs:

- Chicken
- Duck
- Quail

Dried Peas and Beans:

- Black beans
- Black-eyed peas
- Chickpeas
- Falafel
- Kidney beans
- Lentils
- Mature lima beans
- Navy beans
- Almond butter
- Almonds
- Cashews
- Hazelnuts

Nuts and Seeds:

- Peanuts
- Peanut butter
- Pecans
- Pinto beans

- Pistachios
- Pumpkin seeds
- Sesame seeds
- Soybeans
- Split peas
- Sunflower seeds
- Tofu white beans
- Walnuts

Protein Nutrients

Protein is one of the best energy sources, and it helps build, maintain, and repair muscles, bones, skin, cartilage, blood, and other body tissues. It provides the building blocks needed by vitamins, hormones, and enzymes and is one of the micronutrients to provide you with calories.

- **B Vitamins:** These enable energy release in the body, help the nervous system function properly, build tissues, and help red blood cells form. They include B6, niacin, riboflavin, and thiamin.
- **Vitamin E:** This is a powerful antioxidant that helps protect the essential fatty acids and vitamin A in your body from damage by oxidation. Some of the best sources are almonds, hazelnuts, and sunflower seeds.
- **Iron:** This mineral helps transport oxygen around your bloodstream to your cells and strengthens the immune system, helping your body fight infections. A deficiency in this important mineral can lead to anemia, leaving you tired

and weak. This is common in women of childbearing age, and more meat and beans are needed to shore up their diets. You can now purchase many foods, such as flour and breakfast cereals, which have been fortified with iron. There are two types of iron: heme, which is obtained from animal foods, and nonheme, which comes from plant foods. Heme iron is absorbed better than nonheme, so it is recommended that you eat vitamin-C-rich foods with nonheme iron sources to help it absorb better.

- **Zinc:** This is an essential mineral for boosting the immune system function and biochemical reactions in the body need it.

- **Magnesium:** This mineral helps your muscles release energy and builds your bones.

Vegetarian Choices

Most vegetarians will eat plenty of protein, so long as they eat plenty of beans, nuts, beans, seeds, tofu, nut butter, tempeh, and eggs (unless vegan.) If you eat dairy foods, you are consuming foods classed as complete proteins, which means they have all the amino acids your body needs but can't make. Peas, beans, seeds, and nuts are nearly complete, while most veggies and grains are incomplete, meaning they must be consumed alongside soy foods, milk, beans, or other protein source.

Herbs and Spices

Mediterranean people use a lot of herbs and spices in their food, each providing its own flavors and health benefits:

- **Oregano:** Antibacterial properties and full of antioxidants.
- **Basil:** Antimicrobial and anti-inflammatory properties and one of the most versatile herbs.
- **Garlic:** Great for boosting the immune system and benefitting the cardiovascular system.
- **Rosemary:** Helps improve the digestive system and mental cognition.
- **Cumin:** Helps improve digestion and keep blood sugar under control.
- **Turmeric:** Has antioxidant and anti-inflammatory properties.
- **Sage:** Good for digestive health and has anti-inflammatory properties.
- **Saffron:** One of the most expensive spices, this can help improve cognitive function and mood.

Cheese and Yogurt

These are a regular part of the diet but only in moderation. Both contain high amounts of calcium that befit the heart and bones, but low or no-fat varieties are preferred by those who worry about eating too much dairy. Full-fat versions are fine, so long as you keep them to the minimum.

Wine

Regularly consumed in moderation, red wine is typically only drunk with meals unless religious beliefs forbid it. Moderation means women should have no more than a glass (five ounces) and men no more than two. However, just because the diet says you can drink it, don't feel you have to, especially if you don't really drink.

Water

Regardless of diet or lifestyle, water should always be drunk as it is critical for life. Staying sufficiently hydrated helps your organs function properly, benefits overall health, and provides you with energy. Your weight, height, metabolic rate, and exercise levels will dictate how much you should drink, but, as a minimum, you should aim for at least two liters per day.

Moderation

Moderation is key to a healthy, balanced diet. While you are not restricted from eating anything, you should make the right food choices and moderate your portion sizes. For example, you can have a slice of birthday cake, so long as it is small and you don't go back for seconds – or more!

Healthy Lifestyle Habits

Following the Mediterranean Diet is a great step towards good health but must be accompanied by regular physical activity. Strenuous activities, such as running, aerobics, etc., are recommended alongside less strenuous activities, like going for a walk, doing an hour or two of gardening, and even housework – the more you move, the better you will feel.

Mediterranean Diet Principles

Anyone can follow the Mediterranean lifestyle, even if you have food intolerances. You already know the diet principles, as they have all been discussed before, but here they are as your all-in-one, at-a-glance primer:

	PRINCIPLE	WHY
1	**Olive oil should be your main healthy fat source.**	Include 3 to 4 tbsps of extra virgin olive oil daily and benefit from antioxidants called polyphenols in the following ways: • Reduce cancer risk • Help prevent cardiovascular disease • Protect the blood vessels and arteries • Better bone health
2	**Include vegetables with all meals.**	Vegetables are packed with fiber, minerals, vitamins, folic acid, and other essential nutrients. They contain flavonoids that benefit your cognitive functioning and mood, and plant-based diets are also proven to increase longevity and decrease the risks of disease. A flavonoid called allicin is found

		in herbs, spices, onions, and garlic, and this benefits cognitive functioning and the cardiovascular system. Vegetables that contain high levels of calcium, magnesium, and potassium help lower blood pressure.
3	**Eat legume meals at least twice a week.**	Dried and canned legumes are high in fiber, B vitamins, proteins, calcium, zinc, iron, selenium, magnesium, potassium, copper, and phosphorus. That makes them the perfect meat alternative, and they reduce the risk of type 2 diabetes and cardiovascular disease.
4	**Eat shellfish or fish three times weekly.**	These contain high levels of omega-3 long-chain polyunsaturated fatty acids that help regulate heart health and neural functioning. They also help reduce inflammation in the body.
5	**Cut down on red meat.**	Meat is a good source of zinc, selenium, iron, and bioavailable vitamin B12. However, eating

		too much of it can lead to serious health issues. If you must eat red meat, keep your consumption to a minimum and choose free-range, lean, organic meat. Alternatively, replace it with white meat, legumes, and fish.
6	**Eat fresh fruit every day.**	Fruit is one of the healthiest and easiest snacks, and two servings will give you a high level of fiber, folate, vitamins A, B, and C, and flavonoids that protect against the oxidation that causes early aging.
7	**Eat nuts daily and snack on dried fruits**	30 grams of nuts (one serving) provides you with fiber, healthy fat, selenium, vitamin C, vitamin E, antioxidants, and magnesium, all of which reduce your risks of heart disease and fight oxidation.
8	**Eat some dairy every day.**	Two servings per day, especially fermented dairy like Greek yogurt, provide you with vitamins A, B12, and D, calcium, phosphorus, potassium, zinc, and lactic acid bacteria, all helping to lower your risks of colon cancer and improve your gut health.

9	**Moderate your cheese intake.**	If you do eat cheese, choose fermented versions like feta. These contain bioactive compounds that boost your immune system and improve gut health. Eat three 30-gram servings per week.
10	**Eat wholegrain cereals and bread.**	Whole grain foods provide fermentable carbs such as oligosaccharides, resistant starch, and fiber, alongside B vitamins, antioxidants, vitamin E, magnesium, iron, selenium, and copper, all helping protect against obesity, heart disease, and type 2 diabetes.
		Fiber is classed as an indigestible carb. When your gut bacteria is healthy, it breaks these carbs down into short-chain fatty acids, giving your gut cells plenty of energy. These acids also help protect against type 2 diabetes, heart disease, obesity, and other conditions caused by inflammation.

11	**Keep sweets to a minimum.**	You can make your own desserts using healthy ingredients, such as milk, olive oil, and nuts, but you should still keep your consumption to a minimum. Too many sweets can affect your liver's health and functioning, leading to poor overall health.
12	**Eat eggs three times weekly.**	Omega- or free-range eggs provide protein, selenium, choline, phosphorus, riboflavin, and fat-soluble intake. They are also packed with omega-3 fatty acids and other micronutrients that keep your eyes healthy as you age.

Don't forget that socialization is a key aspect of the Mediterranean diet, and meals tend to be a big social occasion, eaten around a large table where everyone joins in. Having a drink may be a part of this, but choose red wine over anything else. That's because it is full of antioxidants, which are not present in other wines or spirits. Two of those antioxidants are resveratrol, which protects the kidneys and heart, and polyphenols, which protect your gut's mucosal lining.

The Mediterranean Diet is not about any particular ingredient. Instead, it is about eating healthy foods with plenty of flavor. Eating veggies flavored with healthy fats gives you even more antioxidants, and nutrients are better absorbed. For example, use olive oil to cook your tomatoes and increase the absorption of lycopene, which has long been shown to lower the risks of heart disease and cancer.

Using herbs like oregano and lemon balm makes your salads more antioxidant, as dos making a salad dressing from red wine or apple vinegar and extra virgin olive oil. Also, when you use more herbs and spices in your food, you will use less salt. Too much salt can lead to hypertension, which can be life-threatening if not treated.

Mindful Eating

Another Mediterranean practice is mindful eating. Mindfulness requires you to be focused in the present moment, acknowledging every thought, feeling, and sensation. Mindful eating goes beyond you as a person, encompassing the effect everything you eat has on the world and environment. This is the concept that led to the US Dietary Guidelines of 2015 being created, focusing on the health benefits of what you eat and crop sustainably.

So, what is mindful eating?

Mindful eating requires you to focus entirely on every mouthful you eat, and when you master it, you'll find you enjoy your food more and make fewer unhealthy choices. It starts from when you buy your food and continues through cooking and serving it, eating it, and how you feel afterward.

Practice the steps below consistently, and you'll soon be eating mindfully without thinking about it:

1. **It Starts with Your Shopping List:** When you write your shopping list, consider every item and the health benefits it offers. Stick to your list rigidly so you don't impulse-buy, and when you get to the store, stick to the outside edges – that's where the fresh, whole foods are. Don't go near the center where all the processed foods are, and ignore the candy at the check-out counter.

2. **Don't be Overly Hungry When You Sit Down to Eat:** You should have an appetite but not so much of one that you gulp your food without tasting it.

3. **Start Small:** Serve a smaller meal on a small plate – smaller plates fool your brain into thinking you are eating a bigger meal.

4. **Learn to Appreciate Your Food:** Before you eat, pause. Take in everything on your plate, around you, and the people who brought that meal to your table or joined you in eating it. Be silently grateful for being able to enjoy a delicious meal and the people with you.

5. **Use All Your Senses:** Whether you cook, serve, or eat, be attentive to everything. As you prepare and eat, take in the textures, color, aroma, and sounds each food makes. As you chew, try to identify every flavor, especially the herbs, spices, and oils used as seasoning.

6. **Eat Small Bites:** You can taste your food better when you take smaller bites. As you take a bite, Put your knife and fork down and experience all the sensations of that mouthful.

7. **Chew Every Bite Thoroughly:** Chew every mouthful until you can truly taste it. That could mean chewing 20 to 40 times, depending on what you are eating. You might just be surprised at all the different flavors you can taste.

8. **Eat Slowly:** Following the steps above should stop you from bolting down your food. Try to take around 20 minutes to eat a meal, enjoying every mouthful and taking in all the flavors released into your mouth.

The next few chapters are devoted to bringing you some of the most delicious recipes, showing you that a diet does not have to be boring or rigid. Instead, you can enjoy amazing flavors in truly satisfying meals.

CHAPTER 4

QUICK AND EASY MEDITERRANEAN BREAKFASTS

A good, healthy breakfast is the best way to start the day, providing you with energy for the day and a good boost of nutrients to keep you going.

Feta and Pepper Omelet Muffins

Total Time: 50 minutes

Serves: 6

Ingredients:

- Cooking spray
- ¾ cup of diced onion
- ¾ cup of crumbled feta cheese
- 2 cups of chopped spinach leaves
- ½ cup of low-fat milk
- ¼ cup of sliced Kalamata olives
- 1 diced red bell pepper

- 8 whole eggs

- 2 tbsp of extra virgin olive oil

- 1 tbsp of chopped fresh oregano

- ½ tsp of ground pepper

- ¼ tsp of salt

Instructions:

1. Preheat your oven to 325°F and spray cooking spray over a 12-cup muffin tray or two 6-cup trays.

2. Heat a skillet over medium heat and add the olive oil. When it is shimmering, add half of the salt and the onion, stir well, and cook for about three minutes or until the onion has begun to soften.

3. Add the oregano and pepper, stir, and cook for four to five minutes, until the vegetables are starting to brown and turn tender. Take the pan off the heat and set it aside for five minutes.

4. Whisk the milk, eggs, pepper, feta, and the rest of the salt. Add the olives, spinach, and cooked veggies, stir to combine, and pour it into the 12 muffin cups.

5. Bake for about 25 minutes or until the eggs have set. Remove from the oven and set aside to cool before removing them from the cups.

6. Once fully cooled, store in an airtight container in the refrigerator.

Nutritional Facts Per Serving (2 muffins):

- Calories: 226
- Carbohydrates: 7 g
- Fiber: 1 g
- Protein: 13 g
- Fat: 17 g
- Sugars: 4 g

Lemon-Blueberry Yogurt Toast

Total Time: 20 minutes

Serves: 2

Ingredients:

- 1 whole egg
- 2 slices of ½-inch thick whole-grain bread
- ¼ cup of fresh blueberries
- 3 tbsp of Greek-style yogurt
- 1 tbsp of organic maple syrup
- 1 tsp of fresh lemon juice
- 1 tsp of fresh lemon zest
- A pinch of salt

Instructions:

1. Preheat your oven to 375°F and place parchment paper on a baking sheet.

2. Whisk the egg, syrup, yogurt, juice, salt, and zest.

3. Lay the bread on the baking sheet and use a dessert spoon to make a flattened well in the center of each piece, leaving a border of about ½-inch all the way around.

4. Divide the yogurt mixture between the two wells and spread it out evenly. Add blueberries on top and bake for about eight to ten minutes, or until the blueberries start bursting and the yogurt mixture is set.

5. Let it cool for about five minutes before serving.

You can also cook this in your air fryer:

1. Line the air fryer basket with aluminum foil, ensuring it rises at least two inches up the sides.

2. Preheat it to 350°F for about five minutes.

3. Follow the oven instructions to prepare the bread and yogurt mixture.

4. Lay the break in the basket and cook for six to eight minutes until the yogurt has set and the berries are bursting. Use the foil to lift the toast from the basket and let it cool for five minutes.

Nutritional Facts Per Serving (1 slice):

- Calories: 167

- Carbohydrates: 23 g

- Fiber: 2 g

- Protein: 9 g
- Fat: 5 g
- Sugars: 10 g

Overnight Berry Muesli

Total Time: 8 hours

Serves: 4

Ingredients:

- 1 cup of muesli
- 2 cups of mixed frozen berries
- 2 cups of plain kefir

Instructions:

1. Divide the muesli between four Mason or similar jars. Add a half-cup of kefir on top and then a half-cup of berries.

2. Stir to combine, put the lid on, and refrigerate overnight.

3. This can be left in the fridge for up to four days.

4. Stir well before you serve it.

Nutritional Facts Per Serving (1 jar):

- Calories: 220
- Carbohydrates: 35 g
- Fiber: 6 g
- Protein: 9 g
- Fat: 8 g
- Sugars: 14 g

White Bean Shakshuka

Total Time: 40 minutes

Serves: 4

Ingredients:

- 2 tbsp of extra virgin olive oil
- 28-ounce can of diced tomatoes in juice
- 15-ounce can of drained, rinsed cannellini beans
- 4 whole eggs
- ¼ cup of chopped fresh dill
- ¼ cup of chopped fresh parsley
- 1 large green bell pepper
- 1 medium yellow onion

- 1 large red bell pepper
- 2 whole garlic cloves
- 1 tsp of paprika
- 1 tsp of ground coriander
- ½ tsp of red pepper flakes (or Aleppo pepper)
- ½ tsp of cumin
- Salt and pepper for seasoning

Instructions:

1. Core and chop the peppers, and mince the garlic. Peel and cut the onion in half and slice it thinly.

2. Heat the oil in a large saucepan over medium-high heat until it is shimmering.

3. Cook the garlic, peppers, and onions until starting to soften, then add the red pepper, paprika, coriander, and cumin. Season with salt and pepper and cook for about five to seven minutes, until the veggies are softer. Stir frequently.

4. Add the tomatoes (including the juices) and the beans. Bring it to a boil, reduce the heat, and put the lid three-quarters of the way over the pan. Simmer for 20 minutes or until the sauce has started to thicken.

5. Take the lid off and use the back of a spoon to push four wells into the sauce, evenly spaced. Crack an egg into each well, making sure it is fairly deep in the sauce. Put the lid back on and cook for five minutes over low to medium heat until the whites are set and the yolk is runny.

6. Take the pan from the heat, drizzle with a little olive oil, and scatter the herbs over the top. Serve straight away.

Notes:

If you follow a vegan lifestyle, just leave the eggs out.

Cannellini beans can be swapped for other mild legumes, like chickpeas, navy beans, butter beans, or Great Northern beans.

Nutritional Facts Per Serving (quarter of the recipe):

- Calories: 114.7

- Carbohydrates: 11.9 g

- Fiber: 3.4 g

- Protein: 7.7 g

- Fat: 4.8 g

- Sugars: 5.9 g

Potato Omelet

Total Time: 20 minutes

Servings: 6

Ingredients:

- 2 tbsp of extra virgin olive oil
- 3 gold potatoes
- 6 whole eggs
- ½ cup of chopped fresh parsley
- ½ cup of chopped fresh dill
- 1 to 2 green onions
- 1 to 2 whole garlic cloves
- 1 tsp of Aleppo pepper
- 1 tsp of coriander

- ½ tsp of sweet paprika

- ¼ tsp of turmeric

- Kosher salt

Instructions:

1. Preheat your oven to 375°F and set a rack in the middle.

2. Heat a large oven-safe skillet and add 2 tbsp of olive oil. Hat until it is shimmering but hasn't started smoking. Meanwhile, peel the potatoes and cut them into even cubes. Chop the onions (white and green bits) and the garlic.

3. Add the potatoes, onion, and garlic, and stir in the salt, Aleppo pepper, coriander, turmeric, and paprika. Cook for five to ten minutes, stirring regularly, until the potatoes are softer and cooked. Be careful not to burn the garlic.

4. Whisk the eggs and herbs together, season generously with kosher salt, and add about ¼ tsp of baking powder if you like – this is optional but makes the eggs a little fluffier.

5. Pour it over the potatoes and cook until the bottom and edges have settled, about three to four minutes.

6. Place the skillet in the oven and bake for eight to ten minutes, until the eggs are fully cooked and no longer runny. Allow to cool to room temperature before serving.

Notes:

You can make this into a lunch or dinner dish by serving it with a salad or vegetables. Leftovers can be stored in the refrigerator for up to four days in an airtight container. Reheat in a hot oven for about five minutes until heated all the way through, or eat cold.

Nutritional Facts Per Serving (one-sixth of the recipe):

- Calories: 176.2
- Carbohydrates: 16.4 g
- Fiber: 2.4 g
- Protein: 7.7 g
- Fat: 9.1 g
- Sugars: 1 g

Menemen (Turkish Scrambled Eggs and Tomatoes)

Total Time: 25 minutes

Serves: 4

Ingredients:

- 1 chopped medium yellow onion
- 1 cored, deseeded, and chopped green bell pepper
- 2 vine-ripened tomatoes
- 4 whole eggs
- 3 tbsp of tomato paste
- 2 tbsp of extra virgin olive oil
- 1 tsp of Aleppo pepper
- ½ tsp of dried oregano

- Salt and pepper

- Crushed red pepper flakes

Instructions:

1. Heat the olive oil until shimmering in a large skillet over medium heat. Cook the onions and peppers, seasoned with salt, for four to five minutes, until soft but not brown. Stir frequently.

2. Add the whole tomatoes and the paste, and season with salt, pepper, Aleppo pepper, and oregano. Stir and cook over medium heat for a few minutes, until the tomatoes start to soften but don't lose shape.

3. Push everything to one side of the pan and turn the heat down to medium-low. Beat the egg and add it to the pan. Stir gently from time to time and cook until just set. Fold it into the tomato mixture.

4. Gently stir a little olive oil in, season with crushed red pepper and Aleppo pepper, and serve hot.

Nutritional Facts Per Serving (quarter of the recipe):

- Calories: 167.4

- Carbohydrates: 9.3 g

- Fiber: 2.5 g

- Protein: 7.2 g

- Fat: 11.5 g

- Sugars: 5.2 g

Loaded Mediterranean Omelet

Total Time: 5 minutes

Serves: 2

Ingredients:

- 4 whole eggs
- 2 tbsp of nonfat milk
- ½ tsp of Spanish paprika
- ¼ tsp of ground allspice
- ¼ tsp of baking powder – OPTIONAL
- 1 ½ tsp of extra virgin olive oil
- Salt and pepper

Toppings:

- ½ cup of halved cherry tomatoes

- 2 tbsp of sliced Kalamata olives

- ¼ to 1/3 cup of drained marinated artichoke hearts, cut into quarters

- 2 tbsp of chopped fresh mint + extra

- 2 tbsp of chopped fresh parsley + extra

- Crumbled feta cheese – OPTIONAL

Instructions:

1. Heat the olive oil in a large skillet over medium-high heat until shimmering.

2. Meanwhile, whisk the eggs, spices, baking powder, milk, salt and pepper.

3. Pour it into the skillet and stir with a silicon spatula for five seconds. Move the cooked parts to the middle, allowing the uncooked eggs to settle around the edge – tilt the pan to make sure the eggs cover the pan.

4. When there is no more raw egg mixture, let it cook for about a minute until the eggs are nearly set and the bottom has gone golden brown.

5. Take the pan off the heat and spoon some of the toppings into the middle third. Fold the omelet, add the rest of the toppings, and garnish with fresh herbs.

6. Slice in half and serve hot.

Nutritional Facts Per Serving (half the omelet):

- Calories: 168
- Carbohydrates: 4 g
- Fiber: 3 g
- Protein: 13.8 g
- Fat: 10.7 g
- Sugars: 1.8 g

CHAPTER 5

LIGHT AND FLAVORFUL MEDITERRANEAN LUNCHES

A light lunch, filled with flavor and delicious ingredients, is the best way to break your day and boost your body with the nutrients you need to keep going.

Avocado Tuna Salad

Total Time: 15 minutes

Serves: 6

Ingredients:

- 3 tbsp of extra virgin olive oil
- 2 tbsp of fresh lemon juice
- 2 chopped avocadoes
- 4 cups of romaine hearts
- 2 cans of drained, flaked solid tuna in oil (5 ounces each)
- 1 cup of chopped English cucumber
- 1/3 cup of crumbled feta cheese
- ¼ cup of chopped Kalamata olives

- ¼ cup of sliced toasted almonds

- 3 tbsp of chopped flat-leaf parsley

- ¼ tsp of salt

Instructions:

1. Whisk the lemon juice, salt, and oil in a bowl.

2. Put the chopped avocadoes in and toss to coat them in the dressing.

3. Next, add the romaine, tuna, almonds, feta, parsley, and olives, and toss to coat and combine.

4. Serve straight away or chill for no more than an hour before eating.

Nutritional Facts Per Serving (a sixth of the recipe):

- Calories: 338

- Carbohydrates: 10 g

- Fiber: 6 g

- Protein: 17 g

- Fat: 27 g

- Sugars: 2 g

Chicken and Veggie Quesadilla

Total Time: 20 minutes

Serves: 1

Ingredients:

- ¼ cup of red bell pepper, diced
- ¼ cup of onion, roughly chopped
- ¼ cup of zucchini, diced
- 2 ounces of cooked, shredded chicken
- 2 tbsp of corn kernels – fresh or canned
- 1 tbsp of fresh cilantro, chopped – OPTIONAL
- 3 tbsp of pepper Jack cheese, shredded
- 1 whole-wheat tortilla, 8-inch
- 2 tsp of Canola oil

Instructions:

1. Heat a skillet over medium heat and add the oil. When it is shimmering, cook the zucchini, pepper, and onion, stirring frequently, for about three to four minutes. The veggies should be tender.

2. Add the corn and chicken and cook for about a minute, stirring frequently, until the chicken is hot. If you are using cilantro, stir it in.

3. Transfer the mixture to a bowl and clean the skillet.

4. Lay the tortilla on a board and sprinkle 1 tbsp of cheese on one half, leaving a gap of ½-inch around the edge.

5. Add the veggie mixture and the cheese, and fold the tortilla.

6. Heat the skillet, add the tortilla, and cook for about two minutes on each side. The cheese should be melting, and the tortilla should be browned all over.

7. Slice into three and serve.

Nutritional Facts Per Serving:

- Calories: 436
- Carbohydrates: 36 g
- Fiber: 4 g
- Protein: 26 g
- Fat: 21 g
- Sugars: 8 g

Vegetarian Power Salad with Creamy Dressing

Total Time: 25 minutes

Serves: 4

Ingredients:

- ½ cup of fresh cilantro, chopped
- ¼ cup of buttermilk
- ¼ cup of low-fat mayonnaise
- 6 cups of lettuce leaves, torn
- 2 cups of kale with stems, finely sliced
- 2 medium carrots, sliced
- 1 can of chickpeas, drained and rinsed (15 ounces)
- 1 cup of quinoa, cooked

- 1/3 cup of unsalted pepitas, roasted

- 1 yellow or red bell pepper, diced

- 2 tbsp of shallot, finely chopped

- 1 tbsp of apple cider vinegar

- ½ tsp of ground black pepper

- ¼ tsp of salt

Instructions:

1. Put the mayonnaise, buttermilk, cilantro, vinegar, shallot, pepper, and salt in a blender and blend to a smooth consistency.

2. Put the kale, lettuce, carrots, chickpeas, pepper, and cooked quinoa in a large bowl.

3. Add the dressing, toss to coat, and serve garnished with pepitas.

Nutritional Facts Per Serving (quarter of the recipe):

- Calories: 362

- Carbohydrates: 38 g

- Fiber: 9 g

- Protein: 13 g

- Fat: 17 g

- Sugars: 6 g

Green Goddess Chickpea Salad

Total Time: 15 minutes

Serves: 2

Ingredients:

For the Dressing:

- 1 pitted, peeled avocado
- 1 ½ cups of buttermilk
- ¼ cup of chopped herbs – your choice
- 2 tbsp of rice wine vinegar
- ½ tsp of salt

For the Salad:

- 3 cups of romaine lettuce, chopped

- 1 cup of cucumber slices

- 1 can of chickpeas, drained and rinsed (15 ounces)

- ¼ cup of low-fat Swiss cheese, diced

- 6 cherry or grape tomatoes, halved

Instructions:

1. Make the dressing. Puree the buttermilk, avocado, vinegar, herbs, and salt in a blender until smooth.

2. Make the salad. Put the cucumber and lettuce in a bowl and toss with a quarter cup of dressing.

3. Add the chickpeas, tomatoes, and cheese, and serve.

4. The remaining dressing will be okay in the fridge for up to three days.

Nutritional Facts Per Serving (half the recipe):

- Calories: 304

- Carbohydrates: 40 g

- Fiber: 12 g

- Protein: 22 g

- Fat: 8 g

- Sugars: 10 g

Lentil Salad with Feta, Tomatoes, Cucumbers and Olives

Total Time: 15 minutes

Serves: 6

Ingredients:

- 3 cups of brown lentils, cooked

- A pint of cherry tomatoes, multicolored, cut in half

- 1 ½ cups of English cucumber, chopped

- ½ cup of Kalamata olives, roughly chopped

- ½ cup thin red onion slices

- ½ cup of feta cheese, crumbled

- ¼ cup of extra virgin olive oil

- 3 tbsp of red wine vinegar

- 1 tbsp of shallot, finely chopped

- ½ tsp of garlic, minced

- ½ tsp of organic honey

- ½ tsp of ground black pepper

- ½ tsp of salt

Instructions:

1. Put the lentils, feta, onion, olives, cucumber, and tomatoes in a bowl, add ¼ tsp each of salt and pepper, and toss. Set to one side.

2. Whisk the honey, garlic, shallot, vinegar, and the remaining salt and pepper. Add the oil gradually, whisking all the time until fully combined.

3. Stir the dressing into the salad gently.

4. Serve immediately.

5. This salad can be stored in the fridge, covered, for up to five days.

Nutritional Facts Per Serving (one-sixth of the recipe):

- Calories: 271

- Carbohydrates: 25 g

- Fiber: 8 g

- Protein: 11 g

- Fat: 15 g

- Sugars: 5 g

Vegetarian Protein Bowl

Total Time: 1 hour

Serves: 4

Ingredients:

- 8 cups of water
- 1 ¼ cups of farro
- 1 can of no-added-salt cannellini beans, drained and rinsed (15 ounces)
- 4 cups of cauliflower florets
- 1 lb. of peeled, cubed sweet potato
- 6 ounces of fresh broccolini, chopped into 2-inch bits
- ½ cup of flat-leaf parsley, chopped
- ¼ cup of cilantro, chopped

- ¼ cup + 2 tbsp of extra virgin olive oil
- ¼ cup of Castelvetrano olives
- 1 tbsp of red wine vinegar
- 1 grated garlic clove
- 2 tsp of lemon-pepper seasoning
- ¾ tsp of salt
- ½ tsp of crushed red pepper flakes

Instructions:

1. Preheat your oven to 425°F and place parchment paper on a large baking sheet.

2. Heat the water to a boil over medium-high, add the farro, and stir. Let it come back to a boil, turn the heat to medium, and leave it to cook for about 30 minutes until the grains have absorbed enough water to expand but haven't softened too much. Add the beans after 25 minutes and stir them in. Drain the mixture and set aside, covered to keep it warm.

3. Put the sweet potato and cauliflower in a bowl. Mix 1 ½ tbsp of olive oil, 1 ½ tsp of lemon pepper, and ¼ tsp of salt and toss the veggies in it. Spread them evenly on the baking tray and roast for 20 minutes or until nearly tender.

4. Put the broccolini in the bowl with ½ tsp of lemon pepper seasoning and 1//2 tbsp of oil, toss, and set aside.

5. Remove the veggies from the oven, push them to one side, and put the broccolini on the other side. Roast for 10 minutes until the veggies are softer and a little charred.

6. Mix the rest of the olive oil with ½ tsp of salt, red pepper flakes, cilantro, parsley, garlic, vinegar, and olives. Add ¼ cup to the farro and stir it in.

7. Divide between four bowls, add the roasted veggies, and drizzle with the rest of the sauce.

8. Serve immediately.

Nutritional Facts Per Serving (quarter of the recipe):

- Calories: 572

- Carbohydrates: 78 g

- Fiber: 13 g

- Protein: 17 g

- Fat: 24 g

- Sugars: 7 g

Chickpea Salad Sandwich

Total Time: 10 minutes

Serves: 4

Ingredients:

- 8 slices of toasted whole-grain bread
- 4 lettuce leaves
- 4 slices of red onion
- 4 slices of tomato
- 4 tbsp of vegan mayonnaise
- 2 cans of no-added-salt chickpeas, drained and rinsed (15 ounces each)
- ½ cup of celery, finely chopped
- ¼ cup of fresh dill, finely chopped

- 6 tbsp of extra virgin olive oil

- 3 tbsp of lemon juice

- 2 tsp of Dijon mustard

- ½ tsp of garlic powder

- 1/8 tsp of ground pepper

- 1/8 tsp of salt

Instructions:

1. Mix the chickpeas with the mustard, lemon juice, oil, and garlic powder. Mash them until just a few chickpeas are left whole.

2. Add the dill, celery, pepper, and salt, and stir to combine.

3. Spread the mayonnaise on one side of each piece of toast and divide the lettuce, onion, and tomato among them. Top with chickpea and finish with another slice of toast.

4. Serve immediately.

Nutritional Facts Per Serving (1 sandwich):

- Calories: 623

- Carbohydrates: 58 g

- Fiber: 12 g

- Protein: 18 g

- Fat: 35 g

- Sugars: 7 g

CHAPTER 6

WHOLESOME MEDITERRANEAN DINNERS

What better way to end the working day than with a wholesome, filling meal served at the dinner table, surrounded by your family and friends?

Salmon Rice Bowl

Total Time: 25 minutes

Serves: 2

Ingredients:

- 4 ounces of wild-caught salmon
- 1 cup of brown rice
- 1 cup of water
- ½ a chopped ripe avocado
- ½ cup of cucumber, chopped
- ¼ cup of spicy kimchi
- 2 tbsp of low-fat mayonnaise
- 1 ½ tsp of low-salt tamari

- 1 ½ tsp of Sriracha
- 1 tsp of avocado oil
- 1 tsp of mirin
- ½ tsp of fresh ginger, grated
- ¼ tsp of red pepper flakes
- 1/8 tsp of kosher salt
- 12 nori sheets

Instructions:

1. Preheat your oven to 400°F and place aluminum foil on a small baking sheet.
2. Put the salmon on the tray and sprinkle with oil and salt. Bake for about eight to ten minutes or until the salmon is flaky.
3. While the salmon cooks put the water and rice in a pan and cook as per the packet directions.
4. Combine the Sriracha and mayonnaise and set aside. Whisk the mirin, tamari, pepper flakes, ginger, and salt in another bowl.
5. Serve the rice in two bowls, topped with salmon, cucumber, avocado, and kimchi. Add the tamari and mayonnaise mixtures, stir, and serve with nori sheets.

Nutritional Facts Per Serving (half the recipe):

- Calories: 481
- Carbohydrates: 47 g
- Fiber: 6 g

- Protein: 18 g
- Fat: 25 g
- Sugars: 3 g

Balsamic Mushroom and Spinach Pasta

Total Time: 20 minutes

Serves: 6

Ingredients:

- 8 ounces of whole-wheat linguine or fettuccine
- 1 lb. of sliced cremini mushrooms
- ¼ cup of fresh basil, chopped
- 4 tbsp of extra virgin olive oil
- 1 ½ tbsp of thin slices of garlic
- 3 ounces of baby spinach leaves
- 3 tbsp of balsamic vinegar
- 2 tsp of vegetarian Worcestershire sauce

- ¾ tsp of salt

- ½ tsp of ground black pepper

- 6 tbsp of unsalted pistachios, roasted

Instructions:

1. Heat a large pot of water to a boil and cook the pasta per the packet instructions. Drain it, keeping the cooking water for later.

2. Heat 2 tbsp of olive oil over medium-high heat and cook the mushrooms for about ten minutes, stirring occasionally. Add the garlic and cook for half a minute, stirring frequently until the garlic is fragrant. Add the spinach and cook until wilted, about a minute.

3. Turn the heat down and add the vinegar. Stir in the Worcestershire sauce, pepper, salt, and the rest of the oil. Stir to combine.

4. Toss the pasta in the mixture, add a quarter cup of the cooking water, and stir it in. Take the pan off the heat and stir the basil in. Serve sprinkled with pistachios.

Nutritional Facts Per Serving (One sixth of the recipe):

- Calories: 276

- Carbohydrates: 35 g

- Fiber: 5 g

- Protein: 10 g

- Fat: 14 g

- Sugars: 5 g

Chickpea Dumplings in Curried Tomato Sauce

Total Time: 45 minutes

Serves: 4

Ingredients:

- 1 can of no-added-salt small diced tomatoes with juice (15 ounces)
- 1 can of no-added-salt tomato sauce (15 ounces)
- 1 cup + 2 tbsp of chickpea flour
- 4 cups of spinach or mustard greens, finely chopped
- 1/3 cup + 2 tbsp of canola oil
- ¼ of red onion, finely chopped
- ¼ cup of plain, full-fat yogurt
- ¼ cup of jalapeno or serrano peppers, finely chopped
- 1 tbsp of fresh ginger, minced

- 1 tbsp of curry powder
- 2 tsp of coriander seeds
- 1 tsp of mustard seeds
- 1 tsp of cumin seeds
- ½ tsp + 1/8 tsp of salt

Ingredients:

1. Combine the flour with 1/3 cup of oil, ½ cup of greens, the onion, peppers, yogurt, and ½ tsp of salt, and make 16 dumplings.

2. Heat the rest of the oil over medium-high heat and cook the mustard, cumin, and coriander seeds, covered, for about 30 seconds – they will start popping.

3. Add the ginger and curry powder, stir, and add the tomatoes and tomato sauce. Stir and the rest of the salt and greens. Let the mixture come to a simmer.

4. Place the dumplings in, cover the pan, and cook for about 20 minutes. Now and then, turn the dumplings over and coat them in the sauce.

5. Serve hot.

Nutritional Facts Per Serving (quarter of the recipe):

- Calories: 454
- Carbohydrates: 41 g
- Fiber: 13 g
- Protein: 12 g
- Fat: 29 g
- Sugars: 1 g

Vegetable Bowl with Chicken and Lemon-Tahini Dressing

Total Time: 30 minutes

Serves: 4

Ingredients:

- 1 cup of green beans
- 1 cup of small broccoli florets
- 4 trimmed chicken cutlets (about 4 ounces each)
- 4 cups of kale, thinly sliced
- ½ a red onion, sliced
- 2 cups of brown rice, cooked
- ¼ cup + 2 tbsp of cold water
- ¼ cup of tahini

- ¼ cup of lemon juice
- ¼ cup of fresh cilantro, chopped
- 2 tbsp of extra virgin olive oil
- ½ tsp of kosher salt
- ½ tsp minced garlic
- 2 sliced garlic cloves
- ¼ tsp of ground cumin
- ¼ tsp of ground black pepper

Instructions:

1. Whisk a quarter cup of water and the tahini into a smooth mixture. Whisk in the lemon juice, ¼ tsp of salt, minced garlic, and cumin. Set to one side.

2. Trim the beans, cut them in half, and use the rest of the salt and pepper to season the chicken.

3. Heat 1 tbsp of oil over medium heat and cook the chicken for three to five minutes on each side. It is ready when a meat thermometer inserted into it reads 160°F. Place the chicken on a clean board and place a tent of foil over the top to keep it warm.

4. Wipe the pan out, heat the rest of the oil, and cook the onion for about two minutes, stirring occasionally. Add the garlic, cook for 30 seconds, then add the beans and broccoli. Cook for about two minutes, stirring occasionally, then add the kale and the remaining water. Cover the pan and steam for one to two minutes, until the veggies are crisp-tender.

5. Slice the chicken, divide the rice between four bowls, and top with veggies and chicken. Season with the rest of the dressing and cilantro.

Nutritional Facts Per Serving (a quarter of the recipe):

- Calories: 452

- Carbohydrates: 42 g

- Fiber: 5 g

- Protein: 35 g

- Fat: 18 g

- Sugars: 3 g

Southwestern Cauliflower Rice Bowls with Shrimp and Avocado Crema

Total Time: 30 minutes

Serves: 4

Ingredients:

- 1 lb. of peeled, deveined large shrimp
- 4 cups of cauliflower rice
- 4 sliced scallions
- 1 cup of frozen or fresh corn kernels
- 1 cup of no-added-salt black beans
- 1 pitted and peeled avocado
- ½ cup + 2 tbsp of fresh cilantro, roughly chopped
- 4 tbsp of plain, low-fat yogurt

- 3 tbsp of avocado oil
- 1 tbsp of chipotle chili in adobo, roughly chopped
- 1 tbsp of lime juice
- 2 tbsp of water
- ¾ tsp of garlic powder
- ¾ tsp of ground cumin
- ½ tsp of salt
- Lime wedges to serve

Instructions:

1. Place the shrimp in a bowl with 1 tbsp of oil and the chipotle. Stir and set it aside.

2. Put the avocado in a blender with the yogurt, ½ cup of cilantro, the lime juice, and 1/8th tsp of salt. Blend to an almost smooth consistency.

3. Heat 1 tbsp of oil over medium-high heat and cook the shrimp for about four minutes or until just cooked. Stir occasionally. Place it in a bowl and cover it to keep the heat in.

4. Heat the rest of the oil and add ½ tsp of cumin, ¼ tsp of salt, and ½ tsp of garlic powder, stirring. Add the cauliflower rice, water, and scallions and cook for about five minutes, until tender.

5. Mix the beans with the rest of the garlic powder, cumin, and salt, and mist the corn with the cilantro in another bowl.

6. Serve the cauliflower rice topped with shrimp, corn, beans, and avocado crema.

NOTE

You can make your own cauliflower rice by grating 8 cups of cauliflower florets or using a food processor to chop it until rice-sized.

Nutritional Facts Per Serving (quarter of the recipe):

- Calories: 402
- Carbohydrates: 28 g
- Fiber: 10 g
- Protein: 32 g
- Fat: 20 g
- Sugars: 4 g

Dijon Salmon with Green Bean Pilaf

Total Time: 30 minutes

Serves: 4

Ingredients:

- 1 ½ lb. of wild-caught salmon, skinned and divided into four
- 12 ounces of trimmed, thin green beans or haricot vert, chopped into thirds
- 8 ounces of cooked brown rice
- 3 tbsp of extra virgin olive oil
- 2 tbsp of pine nuts
- 2 tbsp of water
- 2 tbsp of low-fat mayonnaise

- 1 tbsp of minced garlic
- 2 tsp of whole-grain mustard
- ¾ tsp of salt
- ½ tsp of pepper
- 1 small lemon, zested and cut into four
- Chopped parsley for garnish

Instructions:

1. Preheat your oven to 425°F and place aluminum foil or parchment paper on a baking tray.

2. Brush 1 tbsp of oil over the salmon pieces and put them on the baking tray.

3. Mash the salt and garlic using the side of a knife and combine 1 tsp with the mustard, mayonnaise, and ¼ tsp of pepper. Spread the paste over the salmon.

4. Roast for about six to eight minutes per inch of thickness until the salmon is flaky.

5. Heat the rest of the oil over medium-high heat, and add the pine nuts, green beans, zest, garlic paste, and ¼ tsp of pepper. Cook for two to four minutes until the beans are a little tender, then turn the heat down to medium. Add the water and rice and cook for two to three minutes, stirring frequently, until hot through.

6. Divide the pilaf between four bowls topped with salmon and lemon wedges, garnished with parsley.

Nutritional Facts Per Serving (quarter of the recipe):

- Calories: 442
- Carbohydrates: 22 g
- Fiber: 4 g
- Protein: 32 g
- Fat: 25 g
- Sugars: 2 g

Chicken Parmesan and Quinoa Stuffed Peppers

Total Time: 1 hour

Serves: 4

Ingredients:

- 1 cup of rinsed quinoa
- 1 ¼ cups of water
- 3 cups of cooked, shredded chicken breast
- 1 chopped medium onion
- 1 ½ cups of low-salt marinara
- 1/3 cup of grated Parmesan
- ¾ cup of fresh basil, sliced
- 4 red bell peppers – large ones

- 2 ounces of part-skim, low-moisture, shredded mozzarella cheese

- 1 tbsp of olive oil

- 4 minced garlic cloves

Instructions:

1. Preheat your oven to 350°F.

2. Heat the oil over medium-high heat in a saucepan and cook the onion and garlic for four to five minutes until the onion is translucent.

3. Add the quinoa and cook for 30 seconds, stirring, and then add the water. Str, increase the heat, and bring it to a boil. Turn the heat back down, cover the pan, and let it cook for 15 minutes.

4. Take the pan from the heat and set it aside for five minutes. Then stir in the marinara, Parmesan, chicken, and half a cup of basil.

5. Trim the ends off the peppers, remove the membranes and seeds, and set them in a glass baking dish, cut sides facing up. Cover with plastic wrap and cook in the microwave for three minutes on high. Carefully take the plastic wrap off and divide the quinoa mixture between them.

6. Bake for about 15 minutes until the peppers have softened, then sprinkle with mozzarella. Bake for five to seven minutes, until the cheese is melted, and serve sprinkled with the remaining fresh basil.

Nutritional Facts Per Serving (1 stuffed pepper):

- Calories: 559
- Carbohydrates: 49 g
- Fiber: 8 g
- Protein: 48 g
- Fat: 18 g
- Sugars: 13 g

CHAPTER 7

MEDITERRANEAN-INSPIRED SNACKS

S nacking is often prohibited on many diets, but is positively encouraged on the Mediterranean Diet.

Hummus

Total Time: 3 minutes

Serves: 16

Ingredients:

- 2 cans of chickpeas (15 ounces each)
- ½ cup of tahini
- ¼ cup of extra virgin olive oil

- Juice from 2 lemons
- 2 whole garlic cloves
- 1 tsp of cumin
- ½ tsp of kosher salt

For Garnish:

- Chopped fresh parsley
- Paprika
- Extra virgin olive oil

Instructions:

1. Drain the chickpeas and reserve the liquid.
2. Put the chickpeas in a blender with 1/3 cup of the reserved liquid.
3. Add the rest of the ingredients and blitz for at least 30 seconds, depending on your desired texture. Add more liquid as needed.
4. Transfer it to a bowl and garnish.
5. Serve with cut fresh veggies or whole-grain bread

Nutritional Facts Per Serving:

- Calories: 166
- Carbohydrates: 18 g
- Fiber: 5 g
- Protein: 6 g
- Fat: 3 g
- Sugars: 3 g

Fig and Honey Yogurt

Total Time: 5 minutes

Serves: 1

Ingredients:

- 3 sliced dried figs
- 2/3 cup of plain low-fat yogurt
- 2 tsp of organic honey

Instructions:

1. Put the yogurt into a bowl.
2. Arrange the figs on top and drizzle with the honey.

Nutritional Facts Per Serving:

- Calories: 208
- Carbohydrates: 39 g
- Fiber: 3 g
- Protein: 9 g
- Fat: 3 g
- Sugars: 35 g

Avocado Pesto

Total Time: 5 minutes

Serves: 16

Ingredients:

- 2 ripe avocados
- 1 large bunch of fresh basil
- 3 garlic cloves
- ½ cup of hemp seeds or walnuts
- ½ cup of extra virgin olive oil
- 2 tbsp of lemon juice
- ½ tsp of fine sea salt
- Pinch of black pepper

Instructions:

1. Destem the basil, placing the leaves in a blender.
2. Add the avocado flesh, hemp seeds or walnuts, garlic, lemon juice, and salt, and pulse until everything is chopped finely.
3. Add the oil and pulse to a thick paste. Season with pepper, and blend once more.

Nutritional Facts Per Serving:

- Calories: 126
- Carbohydrates: 3 g
- Fiber: 2 g

- Protein: 1 g
- Fat: 13 g
- Sugars: 0 g

Lemon-Parm Popcorn

Total Time: 5 minutes

Serves: 2

Ingredients:

- 3 cups of air-popped plain popcorn
- 1 tbsp of grated Parmesan
- 2 tsp of extra virgin olive oil
- ½ tsp of lemon pepper
- Pinch of sea salt

Instructions:

1. Whisk the salt, lemon pepper, and oil together.
2. Toss the popcorn in it and sprinkle it with Parmesan.
3. Serve straight away.

Nutritional Facts Per Serving:

- Calories: 99
- Carbohydrates: 10 g
- Fiber: 2 g
- Protein: 2 g
- Fat: 6 g
- Sugars: 0 g

Cinnamon Popcorn

Total Time: 15 minutes

Serves: 4

Ingredients:

- 8 cups of plain popcorn, air-popped
- 2 tsp of sugar (or sweetener equivalent) – see Notes
- ½ tsp of ground cinnamon
- Nonstick butter-flavored cooking spray

Instructions:

1. Preheat your oven to 350°F and place a sheet of aluminum foil in a shallow baking pan.
2. Mix the sugar and cinnamon in a small bowl.
3. Coat the popcorn in cooking spray and sprinkle it with the cinnamon and sugar, tossing to coat.
4. Place it in an even layer on the baking tin and bake for about five minutes or until just starting to turn crispy.

NOTE

If you use a sugar substitute, make sure you follow the package instructions to use the amount equivalent to 2 tsp of sugar.

Nutritional Facts Per Serving:

- **Calories**: 71 (63 if using sweetener)
- **Carbohydrates**: 15 g (13 if using sweetener)
- **Fiber**: 3 g

- **Protein**: 2 g
- **Fat**: 1 g
- **Sugars**: 2 g

Caprese Skewers

Total Time: 10 minutes

Serves: 16

Ingredients:

- 16 basil leaves
- 16 mini mozzarella balls
- 16 cherry tomatoes
- Extra virgin olive oil for drizzling
- Ground black pepper and coarse sea salt

Instructions:

1. Thread one mozzarella ball, tomato, and basil leaf onto each of 16 mini skewers.
2. Drizzle the oil over and season with salt and pepper.

Nutritional Facts Per Serving:

- Calories: 46
- Carbohydrates: 1 g
- Fiber: 0 g
- Protein: 3 g
- Fat: 3 g
- Sugars: 0 g

Pistachio and Peach Toast

Total Time: 5 minutes

Serves: 1

Ingredients:

- 1 tbsp of ricotta cheese, partly skimmed
- 1 tsp of organic honey
- 1 slice of toasted whole-wheat bread
- ½ peach, sliced
- 1 tbsp of pistachios, chopped
- 1/8 tsp of cinnamon

Instructions:

1. Mix the cinnamon, ricotta, and half the honey.
2. Spread it evenly on the toast and layer the peach slices on top.
3. Sprinkle with pistachios and drizzle with the rest of the honey.

Nutritional Facts Per Serving:

- Calories: 193
- Carbohydrates: 29 g
- Fiber: 4 g
- Protein: 8 g
- Fat: 6 g
- Sugars: 14 g

Rosemary-Garlic Pecans

Total Time: 1 hour 20 minutes

Serves: 12

Ingredients:

- 3 tbsp of dried rosemary

- 1 egg white

- 2 tsp of garlic salt

- 3 cups of raw pecans

Instructions:

1. Preheat your oven to 250°F.

2. Whisk the rosemary, garlic salt, and egg white, and add the pecans.

3. Toss to coat and spread them on a large baking sheet in one layer.

4. Bake for about 45 minutes, stirring them every quarter of an hour, then remove them from the oven.

5. Set them aside to cool for half an hour, then serve or store.

6. These can be stored for up to two weeks in an airtight container.

Nutritional Facts Per Serving (¼ cup):

- Calories: 175

- Carbohydrates: 4 g

- Fiber: 3 g

- Protein: 3 g
- Fat: 18 g
- Sugars: 1 g

Cranberry-Almond Energy Balls

Total Time: 10 minutes

Serves: 8

Ingredients:

- ½ cup of dried cranberries
- ¾ cup of whole raw almonds
- ¾ cup of old-fashioned rolled oats
- ¼ cup of pitted dates
- 2 tbsp of fresh lemon juice
- 2 tbsp of tahini
- 1 tbsp of organic maple syrup

Instructions:

1. Put the cranberries, almonds, and dates in a food processor and process for 10 to 15 seconds on HIGH until everything is broken down into small bits.

2. Add the tahini, oats, syrup, and lemon juice and process unto a thick paste.

3. Transfer the mixture to a bowl and roll into 24 balls.

4. These will be stored for up to two weeks in an airtight container in the fridge.

NOTE

If you have a gluten intolerance or celiac disease, use oats labeled as gluten-free.

Nutritional Facts Per Serving (3 balls):

- Calories: 170
- Carbohydrates: 22 g
- Fiber: 4 g
- Protein: 4 g
- Fat: 8 g
- Sugars: 12 g

Curried Cashews

Total Time: 50 minutes

Serves: 6 cups

Ingredients:

- 6 tbsp of curry powder
- 6 tbsp of lemon juice
- 6 cups of raw, unsalted cashews
- 4 tsp of kosher salt

Instructions:

1. Preheat your oven to 250°F and place racks in the top and bottom thirds.

2. Whisk the curry powder with the lemon juice and salt and add the cashews, stirring to coat them completely.

3. Spread them on two baking trays and bake for 45 minutes until dry. Toss them every 15 minutes, then set aside to cool completely.

4. These can be stored for up to three weeks in an airtight container.

Nutritional Facts Per Serving (2 tbsp):

- Calories: 101
- Carbohydrates: 6 g
- Fiber: 1 g
- Protein: 3 g
- Fat: 8 g
Sugars: 1 g

CHAPTER 8

DESSERTS WITH A MEDITERRANEAN TWIST

L astly, we come to desserts. Unlike many diets, the Mediterranean Diet does not restrict you from eating desserts, so long as they are made the Mediterranean way. The desserts in this chapter are perfectly acceptable, so long as they fit your daily calorie and macro intake, but do keep them to a minimum, as they are quite high in sugar, no more than three desserts per week.

Torta Caprese (Italian Chocolate Cake)

Total Time: 45 minutes

Serves: 8

Ingredients:

- 11 tbsp of room-temperature, unsalted butter
- 5 ounces of dark chocolate chips, minimum 70% cacao
- 3 large room-temperature eggs
- ¾ cup of almond flour
- 2/3 cup of granulated sugar
- ¼ tsp of salt
- Confectioners sugar

Instructions:

1. Preheat your oven to 350°F. Brush an 8 to 10-inch cake tin with oil and place parchment paper on the bottom.

2. Melt the chocolate using a double boiler or microwave it on LOW power.

3. Beat the sugar, salt, and butter using an electric mixer until thoroughly mixed.

4. Add the almond flour and eggs and beat until combined.

5. Let the chocolate cool a little, then mix it with the batter until a smooth consistency is reached.

6. Pour it into the cake tin and bake until a toothpick comes out clean, about 25 to 30 minutes. Do NOT overbake, as it will crumble.

7. Let the cake cool down, then remove it from the pan. Leave it for at least half an hour before dusting with confectioner's sugar and cutting.

Nutritional Facts Per Serving:

- Calories: 450

- Carbohydrates: 31 g

- Fiber: 3 g

- Protein: 9 g

- Fat: 34 g

- Sugars: 24 g

Cinnamon Walnut Apple Cake

Total Time: 1 hour 20 minutes

Serves: 12

Ingredients:

- 4 whole eggs
- 1 cup + 2 tbsp of brown sugar
- 1 cup of extra virgin olive oil
- 1 cup of milk
- 2 ½ cups of wheat flour
- 4 apples
- ½ cup of chopped walnuts
- ½ cup of raisins
- 3 tbsp of sesame seeds
- 2 tsp of baking powder
- 1 tsp of vanilla extract
- 1 ½ tsp of ground cinnamon

Instructions:

1. Preheat your oven to 375°F and brush olive oil around a 9-inch cake tin.

2. Peel and core the apples, cut them in half, and slice them thinly.

3. Use an electric hand mixer to beat the sugar and eggs for 10 minutes, then add the olive oil and continue beating for three minutes.

4. Add the flour, milk, vanilla, and baking powder, and beat for two minutes.

5. Pour half of the batter into the cake tin.

6. Mix the apple slices with the walnuts, cinnamon, raisins, and 2 tbsp of brown sugar, and pour it on top of the cake batter.

7. Pour on the rest of the batter, sprinkle sesame seeds over the top, and bake for 45 to 50 minutes. It is ready when a toothpick inserted in the center comes out clean.

8. Let it cool completely before slicing.

Nutritional Facts Per Serving:

- Calories: 452

- Carbohydrates: 54 g

- Fiber: 3 g

- Protein: 7 g

- Fat: 25 g

- Sugars: 25 g

Greek Almond Cookies

Total Time: 1 hour

Serves: 36

Ingredients:

For the Cookie Dough:

- 24 ounces of blanched whole almonds
- 2 ½ cups of confectioner's sugar
- 7 egg whites

For the Topping:

- ¾ cup of confectioner's sugar
- 2 ounces of blanched whole almonds
- 1 egg white

Instructions:

1. Make the dough. Put the almonds in a food processor and pulse to a coarse sugar consistency. Transfer them to a bowl, add the sugar and egg whites, and beat well. Cover and chill the dough for at least half an hour.

2. Preheat your oven to 300°F and put parchment paper on baking sheets.

3. Divide the dough into 6 portions of an ounce each and roll them into balls.

4. For the topping, roll each ball in the sugar. Dip the almonds into the egg white one at a time and place one in the middle of each cookie.

5. Space them on the baking sheets – they won't spread much, so don't leave much room between them.

6. Bake them until light brown at the edges, about 14 to 16 minutes. Set them aside to cool completely.

Nutritional Facts Per Serving:

- Calories: 164

- Carbohydrates: 15 g

- Fiber: 2 g

- Protein: 5 g

- Fat: 11 g

- Sugars: 12 g

Portokalopita (Traditional Greek Orange Cake)

Total Time: 1 hour

Serves: 20

Ingredients:

For the Cake:

- 4 whole eggs
- 1 cup of extra virgin olive oil
- 1 cup of white sugar
- 2 cups of strained plain Greek yogurt
- 3 tsp of baking powder
- 1 package of phyllo sheets (about 1 lb.)
- Zest from 2 oranges

For the Syrup:

- 3 cups of fresh orange juice
- 2 cups of sugar

Instructions:

1. Preheat your oven to 350°F and brush olive oil around a 9 x 13-inch baking tin.

2. Make the cake. Use an electric mixer to beat the eggs, sugar, and olive oil until combined. Add the zest, yogurt, and baking powder and continue beating until combined.

3. Crush the phyllo sheets and add them to the batter. Use a silicon spatula to stir them in and spread the batter in the baking tin.

4. Bake until a toothpick inserted in the middle comes out clean, about 45 to 55 minutes. Remove from the oven and set aside to cool completely.

5. Make the syrup. Heat the orange juice and sugar in a pan over high heat until it comes to a boil. Reduce the heat to medium and simmer for about 20 minutes, stirring frequently, until it thickens to a syrupy consistency. Let it cool down.

6. Slice the cake into 20 equal pieces and pour the cooled syrup over the top. The cake will absorb it.

Nutritional Facts Per Serving:

- Calories: 321

- Carbohydrates: 47 g

- Fiber: 1 g

- Protein: 5 g

- Fat: 9 g

- Sugars: 34 g

Basboosa (Lebanese Semolina Cake)

Total Time: 1 hour 15 minutes

Serves: 24

Ingredients:

For the Basboosa:

- 3 cups of coarse semolina
- 1 ½ cups of sugar
- 1 cup of melted ghee
- 3 tbsp of melted butter
- 1 cup of plain yogurt
- 2 tbsp of tahini
- 1/3 cup of whole, peeled raw almonds
- 1 tsp of baking powder
- ½ tsp of baking soda

For the Sugar Syrup:

- 2 cups of sugar
- 1 cup of water
- 1 tsp of lemon juice

Instructions:

1. Make the basboosa. Mix the semolina, baking powder, sugar, salt, and baking soda in a bowl, and add the melted ghee, yogurt, and butter. Use your hands to mix everything together until combined, and set it aside for 15 minutes.

2. Spread the tahini around a circular baking dish and flatten the mixture into it.

3. Use a sharp knife to score the mixture into 24 diamonds and place an almond on each one. Set aside for 10 minutes.

4. Preheat the oven to 350°F and bake the basboosa for around half an hour until it begins to set.

5. Make the syrup while the cake bakes. Heat the sugar, lemon juice and sugar until it comes to a boil. Decrease the heat and simmer it for 10 minutes, then remove the saucepan from the heat and leave it to cool to room temperature.

6. Take the cake from the oven, cut through the score marks you made, and bake for 15 to 20 minutes. The basboosa should be golden brown.

7. Coat with sugar syrup and set aside to cool before serving.

Nutritional Facts Per Serving:

- Calories: 291
- Carbohydrates: 45 g
- Fiber: 1 g
- Protein: 4 g
- Fat: 6 g
- Sugars: 30 g

Italian Fruit Salad

Total Time: 10 minutes

Serves: 4

Ingredients:

- 1 cup of grapes
- 1 cup of strawberries
- 2 kiwis
- 1 pear
- 1 apple
- 1 banana
- 1 ½ tbsp of sugar or organic honey
- 4 tbsp of fresh lemon juice
- A fresh mint sprig

Instructions:

1. Mix the lemon juice and sugar/honey in a bowl until dissolved.

2. Wash and dry the fruit and cut it all into small pieces – do the banana, pear, and apple last, or they will oxidize and turn brown.

3. Combine everything in a bowl with the lemon juice mixture and mint leaves. Stir to combine and serve.

Nutritional Facts Per Serving:

- Calories: 160
- Carbohydrates: 41 g

- Fiber: 6 g
- Protein: 2 g
- Fat: 1 g
- Sugars: 29 g

Breakfast Torta with Jam

Total Time: 45 minutes

Serves: 8

Ingredients:

- 4 cups of all-purpose flour
- 1 cup of sugar
- 2 whole eggs
- 1 cup of salted butter
- 1 1/8 cup of jam – your choice
- 1 tsp of baking powder
- Zest from a lemon
- A pinch of salt

Instructions:

1. Preheat your oven to 350°F and place parchment paper in a 9-inch round cake tin.

2. Mix the flour and sugar with a little salt and make a well in the center. Crack the eggs and sprinkle the lemon zest over the flour.

3. Heat the butter until melted and pour it in. Mix into a dough using clean hands – if it is too hard, crack another egg in, or add a little more flour if too soft.

4. Add half the dough to the prepared tin, spread with the jam, and crumble the rest of the dough over the top.

5. Bake for about 25 minutes until it starts to brown. Let it cool down and harden before serving.

Nutritional Facts Per Serving:

- Calories: 677
- Carbohydrates: 106 g
- Fiber: 2 g
- Protein: 8 g
- Fat: 1 g
- Sugars: 48 g

Italian Chocolate Coffee Cake

Total Time: 50 minutes

Serves: 8

Ingredients:

Dry:

- 2 cups of all-purpose flour
- 2 cups of white sugar
- ½ cup of unsweetened cocoa powder
- 1 tbsp of baking powder
- 1 tsp of ground coffee

Wet:

- 2 cups of plain, full-fat yogurt (not Greek)
- ½ cup of extra virgin olive oil
- 2 eggs
- A pinch of salt

Instructions:

1. Preheat your oven to 350°F and brush olive oil over a 10-inch round cake tin. Dust it with flour and set aside.
2. Sift and whisk the dry ingredients.
3. Beat the wet ingredients for one minute.
4. Add the dry ingredients to the wet, whisking to combine to a silky smooth consistency.

5. Pour the batter into the tin and bake it for 45 to 50 minutes. It is cooked when a toothpick inserted into the middle comes out clean.

6. Serve with a little plain yogurt.

Nutritional Facts Per Serving:

- Calories: 495

- Carbohydrates: 80 g

- Fiber: 3 g

- Protein: 8 g

- Fat: 2 g

- Sugars: 53 g

Greek Lemon Olive Oil Cake

Total Time: 1 hour 15 minutes

Serves: 16

Ingredients:

- 3 cups of all-purpose flour
- 1 ½ cups of sugar
- 1 cup of extra virgin olive oil
- 1 cup of plain Greek yogurt
- 5 egg yolks
- 1 tbsp of unsalted butter
- 3 tsp of baking powder
- 2 tsp of lemon zest
- Confectioner's sugar for dusting

Instructions:

1. Preheat your oven to 350°F and brush olive oil around a 9 x 9-inch baking dish.

2. Whisk the baking powder, flour, and lemon zest in one bowl and beat the olive oil, sugar, and yogurt in another.

3. Beat the egg yolk in a small bowl and add them to the olive oil mixture. Fold them in until you have a smooth mixture, and mix in the flour mixture.

4. Pour the batter into the baking dish and bake for an hour until cooked.

5. Let the cake cool. Melt the butter, brush it over the top of the cake, and dust it with sugar.

Nutritional Facts Per Serving:

- Calories: 309
- Carbohydrates: 38 g
- Fiber: 1 g
- Protein: 5 g
- Fat: 2 g
- Sugars: 19 g

Rosemary Olive Oil Teacakes

Total Time: 1 hour 15 minutes

Serves: 10

Ingredients:

Dry:

- 1 ½ cups of unbleached white wheat flour (or use spelt flour)
- ¾ cup of whole wheat flour (or whole spelt flour)
- ¾ cup of raw cane sugar
- 1 ½ tsp of baking powder
- 1 tsp of salt

Wet:

- 3 eggs
- ¾ cup of whole milk
- 1 cup of extra virgin olive oil
- ¼ cup of chopped fresh rosemary

Instructions:

1. Preheat your oven to 350°F and brush oil over a 4 ½ x 13-inch springform pan.
2. Combine all the dry ingredients in a bowl, ensuring there are no lumps of sugar or flour.
3. Whisk the eggs in another bowl, then whisk in the rosemary, milk, and oil.

4. Fold the wet and dry ingredients together until well combined.

5. Pour the batter into the baking pan, smooth it over, and bake for 55 to 60 minutes. A toothpick inserted in the center should come out clean when it is cooked.

6. Eat hot or allow it to cool to room temperature.

7. Leftovers can be wrapped in plastic wrap and stored in the refrigerator for up to four days.

Nutritional Facts Per Serving:

- Calories: 423
- Carbohydrates: 42 g
- Fiber: 5 g
- Protein: 7 g
- Fat: 3 g
- Sugars: 16 g

CHAPTER 9

HEALTHY MEDITERRANEAN SMOOTHIES

I f you are in a rush and can't find the time to make breakfast, simply whip up one of these smoothies and get all your nutrients in one easy go. They are packed with fruits, veggies, and other healthy ingredients to keep you satiated. Even better, you can have these smoothies as a snack as well.

You can make smoothies in batches and freeze them in freezer and food-safe, airtight containers for up to three months. Just remove it the night before you want it and let it thaw in the fridge.

Red Bean, Cherry, and Date Smoothie

Total Time: 5 minutes

Serves: 2

Ingredients:

- ½ cup of rinsed kidney beans
- 1 cup of pitted, frozen cherries
- 1 cup of soy milk
- ½ cup of fresh spinach
- 3 pitted dates

Instructions:

1. Pour the milk into the blender.
2. Add the rest of the ingredients and blitz to a smooth consistency.
3. Drink cold.

NOTES

- Add a quarter-cup of rolled oats or half a cup of plain Greek yogurt if you prefer your smoothies thicker.
- Choose low-sodium kidney beans to keep your sodium consumption down.

Nutritional Facts Per Serving:

- Calories: 166
- Carbohydrates: 31 g
- Fiber: 6 g

- Protein: 9 g
- Fat: 9 g
- Sugars: 6 g

Sweet Potato and Chocolate Smoothie

Total Time: 35 minutes

Serves: 2

Ingredients:

- 1 peeled, frozen, medium banana
- Flesh from one cooked cooled sweet potato
- 1 ½ cups of ice
- 1 cup of fat-free plain yogurt
- 1 packed cup of spinach
- 4 pitted dates
- 2 tbsp of sugar-free cocoa powder

Instructions:

1. Soak the dates in warm water for 30 minutes.
2. Put everything in a blender and blend on HIGH until you get a smooth consistency.
3. Serve garnished with flax or chia seeds.

Nutritional Facts Per Serving:

- Calories: 234
- Carbohydrates: 50.6 g
- Fiber: 6.6 g
- Protein: 10.5 g
- Fat: 1.3 g
- Sugars: 28.6 g

Sweet Potato and Mango Smoothie

Total Time: 5 minutes

Serves: 2

Ingredients:

- 1 cup of milk – your choice
- ¾ cup of frozen mango chunks
- 2/3 cup of fat-free vanilla Greek yogurt
- 2/3 cup of cooked, mashed sweet potato flesh
- 1/3 cup of chopped cooked or canned beets
- 2 tbsp of organic maple syrup
- 1 tsp of vanilla extract
- ½ tsp of cinnamon

Instructions:

1. Add the milk to the blender.
2. Add all the other ingredients and blend until smooth.
3. Taste and add more ice or syrup as needed.
4. Enjoy cold.

Nutritional Facts Per Serving:

- Calories: 444
- Carbohydrates: 57 g
- Fiber: 4 g

- Protein: 8 g
- Fat: 3 g
- Sugars: 38 g

Chocolate Avocado Weight Loss Smoothie

Total Time: 35 minutes

Serves: 1

Ingredients:

- 1 cup of soy milk
- 1 frozen banana
- 4 tbsp of large oat flakes
- ½ an avocado
- 1 tbsp of natural peanut butter
- 1 tsp of cocoa powder

Instructions:

1. Soak the oats in the milk for half an hour.
2. Pour them into your blender and add the remaining ingredients.
3. Blend until smooth, adding more milk one tbsp at a time if needed.
4. Serve cold

NOTE

If you want it a little sweeter, blend in a couple of dates.

Nutritional Facts Per Serving:

- Calories: 561
- Carbohydrates: 64 g

- Fiber: 14 g
- Protein: 17 g
- Fat: 30 g
- Sugars: 23 g

Peanut Butter Banana Oatmeal Smoothie

Total Time: 5 minutes

Serves: 2

Ingredients:

- ¾ cup of low-fat or plant milk
- ½ cup of nonfat plain yogurt
- ¼ cup of natural peanut butter
- ¼ cup of ice - OPTIONAL
- 1/3 cup of oats
- 1 frozen medium banana
- 1 to 2 tbsp of organic honey
- 2 tbsp of flax seed – OPTIONAL
- 1 tsp of vanilla extract
- ½ tsp of ground cinnamon

Instructions:

1. Pour the milk into the blender.
2. Add the rest of the ingredients and blend for up to a minute until smooth.
3. Serve cold.

Nutritional Facts Per Serving:

- Calories: 456
- Carbohydrates: 47 g

- Fiber: 7 g
- Protein: 22 g
- Fat: 21 g
- Sugars: 22 g

Watermelon Protein Smoothie

Total Time: 5 minutes

Serves: 1

Ingredients:

- ½ cup of cubed watermelon
- ½ cup of cubed tofu
- ½ cup of pitted, frozen cherries
- ½ cup of soy milk
- 1 tbsp of hemp seed

Instructions:

1. Add the milk to your blender, then add all the other ingredients.
2. Blend until smooth, and enjoy straight away.

Nutritional Facts Per Serving:

- Calories: 292
- Carbohydrates: 22 g
- Fiber: 4 g
- Protein: 21 g
- Fat: 14 g
- Sugars: 15 g

Mango, Strawberry, Yogurt Smoothie

Total Time: 10 minutes

Serves: 2

Ingredients:

- 1 whole, peeled banana
- ½ cup of frozen strawberries
- ½ cup of plain Greek yogurt
- ½ of frozen mango chunks
- ¼ cup of milk – your choice
- 1 tbsp of organic honey
- ¼ tsp of ground ginger
- ¼ tsp of ground turmeric

Instructions:

1. Pour the milk into the blender.
2. Add the remaining ingredients and blend on HIGH until smooth.
3. Serve immediately.

Nutritional Facts Per Serving:

- Calories: 171
- Carbohydrates: 35 g
- Fiber: 3 g

- Protein: 7 g

- Fat: 2 g

- Sugars: 26 g

Blueberry Banana Smoothie

Total Time: 5 minutes

Serves: 1

Ingredients:

- ¼ cup of frozen blueberries
- ½ a peeled banana
- ¼ cup of fat-free vanilla yogurt
- ¼ cup of skimmed milk
- ¾ tsp of organic honey
- ½ cup of ice

Instructions:

1. Add the milk and yogurt to the blender.
2. Chop the banana, and add it to the blender with all the other ingredients.
3. Puree to a smooth consistency.
4. If it is too thick, add a little more milk.

Nutritional Facts Per Serving:

- Calories: 161
- Carbohydrates: 35 g
- Fiber: 3 g
- Protein: 3 g
- Fat: 1 g
- Sugars: 20 g

Mediterranean Diet Berry Breakfast Smoothie

Total Time: 10 minutes

Serves: 2

Ingredients:

- 1 ¼ cups of frozen mixed berries
- 8 ounces of nonfat, plain Greek yogurt
- ¼ cup of milk – your choice
- ¼ cup of oats + more to serve
- 1 tsp of organic honey + more to serve

Instructions:

1. Add the milk to the blender first, then add all the other ingredients.
2. Blend to a smooth consistency, adding a little extra milk if it is too thick.
3. Serve topped with oats and honey.

Nutritional Facts Per Serving:

- Calories: 192
- Carbohydrates: 28 g
- Fiber: 3 g
- Protein: 14 g
- Fat: 2 g
- Sugars: 20 g

Kale and Apple Smoothie

Total Time: 10 minutes

Serves: 1

Ingredients:

- 1 ½ cups of baby kale leaves
- 1 large apple
- 1 cup of unsweetened almond milk (or other unsweetened milk of your choice)
- 2 tbsp of cashew or other nut butter
- 2 tsp of organic honey
- 5 to 6 ice cubes

Instructions:

1. Core the apple and chop it roughly – no need to peel it.
2. Place all the ingredients in your blender, starting with the milk, and blend until combined on medium-low.
3. Turn the speed up and blend until smooth.

Nutritional Facts Per Serving:

- Calories: 376
- Carbohydrates: 49 g
- Fiber: 6 g
- Protein: 9 g
- Fat: 19 g
- Sugars: 31 g

CHAPTER 10

MEDITERRANEAN FLAVORS AND SEASONINGS

Mediterranean cuisine is one of the most flavorful in the world, and that's because of the array of herbs and spices used. While you should keep your pantry stocked with a good variety, it's wise to make sure you have the right ones on hand, and some of the most popular ones you should have are as follows:

Popular Mediterranean Herbs and Spices

Aleppo Pepper:

Aleppo pepper is made from dried Halaby peppers and is named after a Syrian city called Aleppo, where it is made. It is coarsely ground, bright red, mildly spicy, and fruity. Aleppo pepper is commonly used in Turkey and Syria and is one of the most important ingredients in muhammara, a Syrian dip made from toasted walnuts and garlic.

Aleppo pepper can flavor veggie dishes, roasted meats, stews, and eggs.

Basil:

One of the most common herbs in the Mediterranean, there are several varieties but the most common is a large-leafed fragrant variation called Genovese. It has a sweet flavor with mint, pepper, and anise undertones. Greek basil has smaller leaves and a lemon flavor, while the purple variety adds plenty of flavor and color to any dish. Dried basil is sweeter and milder than fresh.

Fresh basil goes well with garlic bruschetta and caprese salad, while dried can be used in soups, stews, or meat dishes.

Bay Leaf:

Also called bay laurel, bay leaf has been used for centuries in the Mediterranean. The leaves are large, grey-green, and flat, with a unique aroma and menthol and eucalyptus flavors. They are usually dried and have a sweeter, mellower flavor than fresh, making them the perfect combination with other herbs, like rosemary, thyme, and oregano.

Dried bay leaves work well in Spanish rice, avgolemono soup, and seafood cioppino.

Borage:

Borage has edible leaves and flowers, tasting like sweet cucumber. Their leaves are fuzzy, and the flowers are blue or purple, shaped like stars. You can use the leaves and flowers, dried or fresh.

Borage is used in risotto, salads, soups, sauces, and pasta fillings.

Cinnamon:

Cinnamon is a popular flavoring for cakes, breads, and cookies, but it's also used in many savory Mediterranean dishes. Grown and harvested in Southeast Asia and China, cinnamon imparts a warm, spicy, earthy flavor.

It is used in Moroccan tagines made with lamb, chicken, and beans, Greek tomato sauces with allspice and nutmeg, and is commonly used in Turkish veggie and meat dishes.

Coriander:

In the USA, dried coriander is the seeds from the cilantro plant, harvested and dried. However, in much of the rest of the world, coriander refers to the seeds and fresh leaves. The dried seeds have a mild citrus flavor and are earthy and mellow. Coriander is used in most Mediterranean countries, including Lebanon, Algeria, Morocco, and Greece, and is an important ingredient in garam masala, za'atar, and other spice blends.

Coriander works well in soups, marinades, stews, and other long-cooking dishes.

Cumin:

Cumin seeds have a strong, warm, earthy flavor, slightly bitter, with nutty undertones. It works well with ground coriander and is used in many spice blends, such as the North African Ras el hanout.

Cumin works well in vegetable, seafood, and meat dishes.

Fennel Seed:

Fennel grows well in most Mediterranean countries and has a strong aniseed aroma, tasting mildly of licorice.

Fennel seeds may be ground or used whole in meat rubs, spice blends, and bread and are commonly used in Italy and Greece to flavor lamb or pork sausages. You can also toast whole seeds and use them to garnish soups and veggie dishes.

Lavender:

Lavender has a strong aroma and floral flavor, bringing a lovely flavor to some baked goods, desserts, and savory dishes. Edible flower buds can be dried and crushed or used whole, and only a little is needed. It is one of the main ingredients of Herbes de Provence.

Lavender is used to infuse oil in marinades and cheeses and goes well with citrus and honey dishes.

Marjoram:

With a mild, woodsy flavor, marjoram is part of the mint and oregano family. The plants have white flowers and small leaves, and dried marjoram is more intense than fresh. Like lavender, it features heavily in Herbes de Provence.

Marjoram goes well with other herbs, like sage, oregano, and rosemary, and is often used in Greek or Italian spice blends for tomato sauce and meat seasonings.

Mint:

More than just an ice cream flavor, mint is hardy, easy to grow, and provides a crisp, cool effect. There are several varieties of mint, each with its own flavors and intensities, including chocolate, pineapple, lemon, orange, and apple varieties, to name just a few.

You can use mint leaves, dried or fresh, in savory and sweet dishes. For example, tabbouleh is a salad made from cold bulgar wheat and full of mint. It is used in tzatziki sauce, fish soup, and many other dishes and also as a garnish or to make fresh mint tea.

Oregano:

One of the most used herbs in Greek cuisine, oregano belongs to the mint family and is a low-growing, spreading plant with tiny flowers and leaves. It has an earthy, grassy aroma with pepper and mint undertones and an unmistakable aroma.

Oregano is used to season pizza and spaghetti sauces and is commonly used in veggie, egg, and meat dishes and salads. It is also included in za'atar and other spice blends from North Africa.

Paprika:

Paprika is made from dried red peppers, ground into powder, with a sweet, hot, or mild flavor, depending on the pepper used and the amount of ribs and seeds that are ground up. Smoked paprika comes from peppers that are smoked whole and ground up.

It is commonly used to garnish dishes but is also used to flavor egg and chicken dishes, sauces, and stews.

Parsley:

Parsley is one of the more versatile herbs and can be used fresh or dried. It has a vibrant, fresh flavor and a beautiful color when used fresh.

Parsley is often used to garnish dishes, holds up when cooked, and is often used with roasted veggies, roast meats, and soups.

Rosemary:

Also belonging to the mint family, rosemary is a woody shrub with a strong smell and flavored with pine, eucalyptus, and camphor notes. You can use it dried or fresh.

Rosemary is commonly used to flavor roast lamb and other meats, roasted potatoes, and vegetables and is often used alongside garlic and lemon. Greek chefs flavor olive oil with rosemary for dipping bread in, and it is also used in Herbes de Provence and bouquet garni.

Saffron:

One of the most expensive spices in the world, saffron comes from a type of crocus and is typically grown in the Mediterranean, India, and the Middle East. The saffron strands are crocus flower stigmas and must be harvested by hand. Each flower has only three stigmas, which means hundreds of crocus flowers are needed to produce a single gram.

It is commonly used in Mediterranean cooking, especially meat and rice dishes. It has an earthy, musky, slightly bitter flavor and gives any dish a golden yellow color. It is used in Moroccan tagines, Italian risotto, and Spanish paella.

Sage:

Sage leaves are aromatic and are a common part of Mediterranean cooking. While you can use fresh leaves, they are mostly dried, as dried sage is much stronger. It has a peppery, earthy flavor and is typically used in Greek sausages, mushroom dishes, and meat marinades. In Italy, it is used to flavor all manner of dishes, and Albanians use it to make soothing teas.

Sumac:

Sumac is fast becoming a popular spice in the USA but has long been used in Mediterranean cooking. It is a shrub with long stems and berry clusters. The ripe berries are dried and ground into a spice with a fruity citrus flavor.

Sumac is used in Lebanon to flavor Fattoush salad, while Palestinians use it to flavor musakhan, a low-roasted chicken dish. It is also used in the za'atar spice blend and goes well with most braised meats, salad dressings, and dips.

Thyme:

Thyme is one of the more revered, an ancient herb used in the entombment of Egyptian pharaohs. These days, it is an important ingredient in many Mediterranean dishes. Thyme is a low-growing spreading plant with minuscule, wonderfully aromatic leaves on creeping stems and is part of the mint family, alongside marjoram, oregano, and rosemary.

With its peppery, lemony flavor, thyme is used in many dishes, including focaccia bread, and is included in many Greek and Italian spice blends, in za'atar and Herbes de Provence.

Za'atar:

Za'atar is a blend of many of the spices and herbs listed above, and it is commonly used in Israel, Lebanon, Syria, and much of the Middle East. The ingredients depend on the country, but the common ingredients are:

- Coriander
- Marjoram
- Oregano
- Salt
- Sumac
- Thyme
- Toasted sesame seeds

It has a herby, earthy flavor with a touch of tang from the sumac.

~ 172 ~

Za'atar is best with vegetables and meats, especially slow-cooker recipes, and is also used as a condiment like pepper and salt. You can dip bread in it, add it to hummus or a yogurt sauce, or sprinkle it over soft cheeses and press it in.

Here are a few blends you can make in your own kitchen. Simply combine all the ingredients and store in an airtight container:

Mediterranean Herb and Spice Mix

Ingredients:

- 2 tsp of dried thyme
- 2 tsp of dried oregano
- 2 tsp of sweet or hot smoked paprika
- 1 ½ tsp of fine kosher or sea salt
- 1 tsp of ground black pepper
- 1 tsp of roasted, ground coriander seeds
- 1 tsp of roasted, ground cumin seeds

Mediterranean Seasoning Blend

Ingredients:

- 1 tbsp of granulated garlic

- 1 tbsp of dried Greek oregano

- 1 tbsp of dried basil

- ½ to ¾ tbsp of fine sea salt

- ½ tbsp of dried parsley

- ½ tbsp of dried dill weed

- ½ tbsp of onion powder

- 1 tsp of dried finely ground rosemary

- 1 tsp of dried thyme

- 1 tsp of coarse ground black pepper

- ½ tsp of dried marjoram – OPTIONAL

- ¼ tsp of ground cinnamon - OPTIONAL

Mediterranean Spice Mix

Ingredients:

- 3 tbsp of dried rosemary
- 2 tbsp of ground coriander
- 2 tbsp of ground cumin
- 1 tbsp of dried oregano
- 2 tsp of ground cinnamon
- ½ tsp of fine salt

Smoky Mediterranean Spice Blend

Ingredients:

- 4 tbsp of smoked paprika
- 4 tbsp of Spanish paprika
- 3 tbsp of ground sumac
- 3 tbsp of granulated garlic powder
- 3 tbsp of onion powder
- 2 tbsp of kosher salt
- 1 tbsp of black pepper
- 3 tsp of toasted and ground cumin seeds

Mediterranean Seasoning

Ingredients:

- 1 tbsp of dried basil
- 1 tbsp of dried oregano
- 1 tbsp of garlic powder
- ½ tbsp of dried parsley
- ½ tbsp of dried dill weed
- 2 tsp of onion powder
- 1 tsp of dried thyme
- 1 tsp of dried rosemary
- 1 tsp of grated lemon peel
- 1 tsp of coarse ground black pepper
- ½ tsp of kosher salt
- ½ tsp of ground cumin – OPTIONAL
- ¼ tsp of ground cinnamon - OPTIONAL

Growing Your Own Herbs

While dried herbs are readily available at every grocery store, many recipes call for fresh. Instead of hunting for them, why not grow your own? Herbs are such a big part of Mediterranean cooking that having your own home-grown herb garden makes sense, so you can simply cut what you need. That way, you know you are using the freshest ingredients.

Even better, you can grow virtually any herb at home. They are easy to grow, and you don't need a garden – most can easily grow in pots on a warm, sunny windowsill. You can grow from seed or buy starter plants from a garden nursery – this is usually the preferred option, as once they are settled in their pots, they can be used almost straight away.

Prepare Your Pots and Soil

First, decide if you are growing them on your patio, terrace, or windowsill, then choose the size pots you want. You can grow them in individual containers or have one large one with several varieties – not mint, though, as it is incredibly invasive and needs its own pot. Make sure the containers have drainage holes and a water tray to stand on.

Combine 50% organic compost with 50% garden soil, or purchase a specific potting soil for herbs and fill your pots. Transplant your herbs into place, water them in, and leave them to settle in.

Once your herbs are planted, you need to care for them.

- **Light:** Herbs love the sun, so make sure they are positioned where they get a good amount. You will need to turn the pots regularly so that the sun reaches all parts of the plant, stopping the herbs from growing in strange shapes as they lean toward the sun. If your stems grow with few leaves, the plant isn't getting sufficient sunlight.

- **Watering:** Hardy herbs need regular water, especially when grown in pots. You need to understand the different watering requirements of each herb. If you choose to grow several in one container, try to ensure they all have similar requirements. Water twice a week, keeping the soil moist but not overly wet, as this can cause the roots to rot. Test the soil by poking your finger in an inch or two – if it is dry all the way down, they need watering.

- **Prune and Harvest:** Encouraging growth is easy; simply clip them regularly, and they will grow. Do this often, but don't prune more than a third of the plant off. If flowers start to appear, you need to prune, so the energy goes into growing the plant, not the flowers. Cut fresh leaves off regularly using scissors, starting at the base of the plant.

Growing herbs at home couldn't be easier, so plant your garden today. The easier it is to get them, the more likely you are to use them in your cooking.

Essential Techniques for Authentic Mediterranean Cooking

Mediterranean cuisine is about more than the food. It's about how you prepare and cook it. Familiarize yourself with the common methods and experiment to bring your own touch to every dish you cook.

Slow Cooking

Slow cooking is one of the most used cooking methods in the Mediterranean, allowing the food to cook for a long time and blending the flavors. This ensures every tender mouthful is an explosion of flavor. Common Mediterranean dishes are slow-roasted lamb shoulder, Beef goulash, and braised lamb shanks.

Pro Tips:

- **Keep the heat consistent.** Low, steady heat ensures the food doesn't overcook or burn and keeps it tender and full of flavor.
- **The right cooking pot.** This is usually a Dutch oven or heavy-bottomed pot as these ensure the heat is evenly distributed, although you can use a modern electric slow cooker.
- **Intentional layering.** Always put the ingredients that take the longest to cook at the bottom and layer up to those that take the least time.
- **Use fresh herbs.** Slow-cooking fresh herbs allows their flavors to infuse with the rest of the food, imparting a wonderful flavor.

- **Don't overcrowd the pan.** Too much food stops the food from breathing and cooking evenly.
- **Seal it well.** This keeps the moisture in, allowing for better flavors.
- **Be patient.** Don't keep taking the lid off to check the food. This lets heat out and slows the process even further. Be patient and your dish will be just fine.

Grilling and Charring

Charring is another popular Mediterranean cooking technique, enveloping foods with a rich, smoky flavor, be it chicken, fish, or vegetables. Grilling is also popular, with many dishes being grilled over open flames.

Pro Tips:

- Char veggies over an open flame to get a deep smoky taste, but use a stove or broiler to have more control over the char.
- Once your veggies are charred, seal them in foil or in a container for 10 minutes. This will steam them, making it easier to remove the skin. Be careful, though, as the veggies will be hot.
- Brush vegetables with olive oil before grilling to stop them drying out. It will also prevent them from sticking to the grill and provide the veggies with an extra depth of flavor, caramelizing them and producing those grill marks.
- Preheat your grill – every time. That ensures the food cooks evenly and gives you the sear marks.

- Know the cooking times of every vegetable, a they are all different. Bell peppers and other dense veggies take longer than zucchini and other soft veggies, so make sure to adjust the grilling time as needed.

Marinating

Marinating is commonly used in Mediterranean cooking, as it helps tenderize meat, fish, and veggies and provides an amazing flavor. Marinating is nothing more complicated than soaking the food in an olive oil-based liquid, with plenty of herbs and spices to impart the flavors.

Pro Tips:

- **Time is important.** Most meats require two to eight hours, while fish only need 30 to 60 minutes. If you leave it too long, the meat may turn to mush, especially if using a vinegar or acid-based marinade.
- **Don't forget the yogurt.** Plain yogurt is a common ingredient in marinades, adding a lovely tang to the food.
- **Use the right containers.** Plastic or glass is best as metal can interact with the acid in the marinade, changing the flavor of the food.
- **Check the temperature.** While you should always place marinating food in the fridge to keep it fresh, you should ensure it comes to room temperature before cooking it. That way, it will cook evenly.

- **Soak the food.** The food must be completely coated in the marinade to ensure even flavoring. Turn it or massage it gently from time to time.

Fermenting and Preserving

Fermenting and preserving are age-old techniques to help bring flavor to food and give it a much longer shelf life. This means that, even when the weather changes and the crops no longer grow, you can still enjoy the harvests of summer, even in the depths of winter. Pickling and fermenting also provide food with amazing flavors. For example, crunchy cucumbers turn into zesty pickles, and whole milk makes the most amazing yogurt with a fresh tang. Lastly, fermented foods are packed with probiotics and are excellent for the digestive system.

Pro Tips:

- Always use clean, sterilized equipment and jars to stop bacteria from spoiling the food.
- Use the highest quality foods. When you bring in the harvest, preserve what you don't eat straight away.
- Be patient. Fermenting and pickling are not quick, sometimes taking weeks or even months before the full flavors are developed.
- Don't be afraid to experiment. Try new spices in your pickles or make jams from different fruits.
- Safety is paramount, so ensure you follow the proper guidelines for fermenting and pickling. These have been developed to ensure your food is safe to eat.

Making Stocks

Stocks are a basic staple in the Mediterranean kitchen. They may look like nothing more than a clear liquid but they are full of flavor, made by simmering bones, meat, fish, or veggies to extract their goodness and flavors. For example, stock made from herbs and fish bones is perfect for a bouillabaisse.

Stocks are also one of the most versatile ingredients. They can help reduce strong flavors, as a base for soups and stews, and even cook grains and add flavor to them.

Stocks are all about zero-waste. Keep your veggie peels, poultry bones, fish heads, etc., and use them to make different flavored stocks.

Pro Tips:

- Simmer your ingredients, as boiling them allows impurities to mix in with the stock. Simmering ensures you get a crystal-clear stock full of goodness and flavor.
- Skim your stock. Check for impurities and foam and skim them off the top regularly, ensuring they don't get incorporated back into the stock.
- Cool your stock quickly to keep it fresh and safe to consume. Once cooled, it must be stored, and one of the easiest ways is to portion it out and freeze it. Ice cube trays are good for this.

Balancing the Flavors

No matter what it is, every Mediterranean dish is packed with flavor, but it's a delicate balance. Be it the citrusy flavor of lemon paired with the savory flavors of lamb or creamy feta and juicy cherry tomatoes, the right balance creates a symphony of flavor in every mouthful.

Learning how to do this takes time and patience, but it's a critical skill to learn if you want to master Mediterranean cooking. Perhaps the best example is the humble Greek salad, a masterful balance of crumbly, salty feta cheese with the sharpness of the olives, the crunchy, juicy cucumber with the juicy tang of cherry tomatoes. The Greek salad may be humble, but it perfectly represents flavor balance.

Pro Tips:

- Taste all the time. When you cook, taste as you add ingredients and seasoning, ensuring each ingredient can shine without the others overpowering it.
- Don't shy away from acid. If your dish feels bland, heavy, or one-dimensional, add a squeeze of lemon or a little vinegar. It can brighten a dish up no end, cutting through rich flavors, and bringing out the flavors of other ingredients.
- Be sparing with the sweetness. Many Mediterranean dishes already have underlying sweet notes, be it from honey, fruits, or some veggies. Be very sparing when adding other sweet ingredients, as they may dominate the dish rather than complement it.

- Use fresh herbs to help balance and bring out other flavors. For example, rosemary goes well with mild ingredients, adding depth, while mint can cut through spicy flavors and temper them a little.
- Use salt wisely. Too much can make a dish too salty, while just enough can bring out other flavors.
- Learn to balance bitter flavors. Some greens, olives, and even olive oil can have a bitter flavor profile, so learn how to balance it with other flavors to bring out the best in your dish.

Don't Skimp on Healthy Fats

Olive oil and ghee are two important ingredients in Mediterranean cooking, and they are two of the healthiest fats you can eat.

Olive Oil:

Olive oil has a slightly bitter, fruity, lightly peppery flavor that can enhance a dish, be it fresh bread dipped in it, a base for a sauce, or drizzled over a salad. It is packed with antioxidants and monounsaturated fats and has been proven to help reduce the risks of heart disease while increasing overall wellness. Always use extra virgin olive oil, as it is the purest form with the most benefits.

Pro Tip:

- Olive oil does not have such a high smoke point as other oils, which means you should never use it for deep frying. Use it drizzled over food, in sauces and dressings, or for sauteing food.

Ghee:

Ghee, otherwise known as clarified butter, is used a great deal in Middle Eastern and Mediterranean cooking. It has a nutty flavor and is easy to make. Simply simmer butter to separate the milk solids and water out, leaving a golden, clear liquid. It also has a high smoke point, so you can use it for high-heat cooking and frying.

Pro Tip:

- Ghee is potent, so you only need to use a little at a time. Melt it over a flatbread for a wonderful flavor, or fry your spices in it.
- Learning these traditions will help you master Mediterranean cooking in no time at all, allowing you to experience the true flavors of every meal you cook.

CHAPTER 11

THE MEDITERRANEAN DIET ON A BUDGET

The Mediterranean Diet is touted as the healthiest diet, and following it can help you keep your weight healthy and reduce your risks of some cancers, diabetes, heart disease, stroke, and other chronic diseases. There are also studies to show it can help improve cognitive functioning and extend your life.

In the current cost-of-living crisis, food prices are creeping up, and most people are looking for ways to cut back. The Mediterranean Diet brings images of expensive olive oil, fresh seafood, and costly red wine to many people's minds, but it doesn't have to be a cost-prohibitive diet. In fact, it is very easy to follow this lifestyle without it costing you an absolute fortune.

It is safe to say that the diet is based on what used to be called "peasant foods." Whole grains, seasonal fruits and vegetables, and legumes are all cheaper than processed foods and meat. That means the Mediterranean Diet is far more affordable than many people realize. Also, eating fewer takeaways and restaurant meals and cooking more at home will save you money, along with eating less red meat.

Top Tips for the Budget-Conscious

Read on for some tips on following the Mediterranean Diet on a budget.

Make Wholegrains a Big Part of Your Meals

Skip the refined white pasta and rice and look for wholegrain versions instead. Use wheat berries, farro, freekeh, bulgar, millet, and spelt in your meals. Most grocery stores will sell these in bulk, which is a cheaper way of buying them than by the box. You can also purchase wholegrain pasta in bulk for about the same price as refined.

Whole grains are one of the Mediterranean Diet's foundation foods, and you can easily create a healthy meal with some wholegrain pasta, a can of tomatoes, a can of beans, and some greens in less than 15 minutes.

Don't Shy Away from Beans

Chickpeas, lentils, and beans are shelf-stable protein sources, an excellent alternative to meat, much healthier and much cheaper. Beans are easy to use:

- Spread hummus on a whole meal wrap and add cut veggies.
- Add a handful of lentils to your Bolognese.
- Ditch the meat in your chili and make it a three-bean one.
- Add cannellini beans or chickpeas into grain or pasta bowls.
- Make burgers and tacos with black beans instead of ground beef.

Canned beans are perfectly healthy and easy to use but dried are even cheaper. You just need to factor in soaking time, but this can be done overnight.

Use Canned Fish

Seafood and fish should be eaten at least twice a week on the Mediterranean Diet, but there's no need to splash out on expensive fresh fish. Use canned salmon, tuna, and sardines instead. They are more affordable and a convenient way of including fish in your diet. Try these tips:

- Add canned tuna to crisp lettuce leaves, tomatoes, olives, cucumber, fresh mint, red onion, and feta cheese for a tasty salad.
- Make a Niçoise salad with lettuce, blanched green beans, tomatoes, olives, eggs, boiled potatoes, and tuna, dressed in a tarragon vinaigrette.
- Make salmon cakes with canned salmon, served on a bed of lettuce or arugula, with a tzatziki sauce.

Don't Buy Pre-Chopped Leafy Greens

Leafy greens are a big part of the diet and Mediterranean people commonly pick and chop their own. Growing your own is easy and takes little space, but if you can't, buy whole bunches of greens at the grocery store instead of pre-chopped versions.

Leafy greens are also about more than kale and spinach. Try mustard greens, beet greens, chicory, escarole, chard, and any other deep-colored leafy green you want. Simple ways to add leafy greens to your diet are:

- A popular Italian dish of white cannellini beans, garlic, and sauteed greens.

- Add a handful of kale to your soups.
- Use it instead of lettuce in a salad.

Fill Your Freezer With Frozen Veggies

While fresh veggies are always preferable, there is nothing wrong with frozen, so long as they don't have added sodium. Frozen veggies are cheaper and just as nutritious, given that they are frozen at peak freshness, sealing in all the flavor and nutrition. They are convenient and eliminate food waste – who hasn't tossed out veggies that have gone off before they can be eaten?

Frozen veggies are the perfect addition to one-pot meals, for serving with grains and for sauteing in olive oil.

Buy Your Poultry Whole

Poultry is recommended in place of red meat on the Mediterranean Diet, although still in moderation. Precut chicken and turkey portions can be expensive, so buy it whole. It usually works out at roughly 50% cheaper per pound than precut.

Cook the whole bird, slice it, and freeze what you don't eat. Some of the underused meat, bits you would normally throw away, can be simmered in a stew with beans and veggies, while the carcass can be used to make stock — half the cost and far less waste.

Buy Your Nuts in Bulk

Nuts are not always cheap to buy but are a Mediterranean Diet staple. They are packed with healthy fat, fiber, protein, and other nutrients you don't get in processed snacks. And they can be added to just about any meal. Almonds, pine nuts, walnuts, hazelnuts, cashews, and hazelnuts are often used in grain dishes, salads, sauces, and dips.

Instead of fretting over the cost of a small bag, see if you can buy them in bulk to save money – do check the prices, though. Purchase unsalted whole nuts and store them in the refrigerator in dark, airtight containers to increase their shelf life.

Make Your Own Salad Dressings

Store-bought salad dressings are expensive and usually full of preservatives, sugar, sodium, and other unhealthy ingredients. Making your own is simple and much healthier, and you likely already have the ingredients – lemon juice, olive oil, balsamic vinegar, herbs, and spices.

A simple dressing can be made by whisking white vinegar and olive oil in equal parts with a little salt, minced fresh garlic, organic honey, and mustard. And you can make it in bulk and store it in the refrigerator for use every day.

Use different fresh or dried herbs; if you don't have fresh garlic, you can use powdered garlic or granules.

Grow Your Own Herbs

Fresh herbs are amazing, packed with flavor and nutrition, and are an important addition to any meal. Rather than buying them at the store, grow your own. You can grow small pots of most herbs and just snip off what you need. That way, there is no waste, and you encourage the plants to keep growing.

Let's look at the best foods for following the diet on a budget, including their health benefits.

Top Twelve Budget Foods for the Mediterranean Diet

Healthy eating requires no small amount of flexibility to ensure that you stick to it for the long term. The Mediterranean Diet is successful because of its flexibility and is one of the easiest to follow. No more rigid rules, no more restrictions. Simply eat more vegetables and fruits, whole grains, lean protein and unsaturated fat, and less processed, sugary foods.

Unlike many fad diets, the Mediterranean Diet doesn't need to be expensive, either. There are plenty of foods you can include that offer great health benefits and are perfectly budget-friendly.

1.   Beans

Beans offer plenty of vitamins, fiber, and minerals sorely lacking in standard Western diets, like iron, magnesium, and potassium. Their protein and fiber content makes them filling and an easy alternative to meat. Eating beans instead of meat a couple of times a week will help you cut your saturated fat consumption.

There are more than 4,000 bean varieties in the USA alone, and each has its own flavor profile. This makes them an incredibly versatile ingredient that can be eaten for any meal. For example:

- Creamy white bean soup made with cannellini beans.
- Slow cooker chicken and pinto bean enchilada casserole.
- Chipotle black-eyed peas and collards with shallots.

You can even add beans to desserts to boost their protein and fiber content and provide a lovely, creamy texture.

Canned beans are cheap, but you should consider bulk-buying dried beans.

2. Peanut Butter

Nuts are full of protein, healthy fats, and fiber, helping keep you fuller for longer. They contain unsaturated fats, which are highly recommended on the Mediterranean Diet and can help reduce inflammation and support your heart and brain.

You can usually pick up a jar of natural peanut butter for a couple of dollars, making it a cost-effective addition to your diet. Use organic or natural where possible, and use it in many different dishes, including those with a peanut sauce.

3. Lentils

Who doesn't love lentils? They are one of the most nutritious foods you can eat, with a third of a cup of cooked lentils containing an impressive 5 grams of fiber, 6 grams of proteins, 13% of your daily iron needs, and 30% of your folate requirements.

Lentils are cheap to buy, usually costing 10 cents or less per serving, and they are one of the quickest-cooking of all dried legumes, taking less than half the time. You can use lentils in many dishes, including soups, stews, salads, and smoothies.

4. Potatoes

Potatoes are such a versatile ingredient and are incredibly nutritious and cheap to buy. They are full of fiber, vitamin C, and potassium (do eat the skin as that's where many nutrients are) and can help support heart health and immune function. They also provide protein and can be used in many different dishes, including pancakes, frittatas, soups, and stews.

5. Canned Fish

As mentioned above, canned fish is cheaper than fresh but no less nutritious. It's also more shelf-stable, pre-cooked, and convenient to use. Add canned fish to salads, casseroles, sandwiches, and more.

6. Canned Tomatoes

Canned tomatoes are picked at their best freshness and canned straight away to preserve the nutrients and flavor. They are much higher in lycopene and iron than fresh tomatoes and are way cheaper, especially if you purchase in bulk. They can be added to just about any dish, from rice and pasta to sauces, stews, curries, soups, and more.

7. Garlic and Onions

Both of these offer plenty of nutrition, including prebiotic fiber that feeds the healthy bacteria in the gut. Garlic can help keep blood pressure stable, boost immune health, and reduce cholesterol, while onions keep blood sugar stable and protect the heart through their anti-inflammatory properties.

You can also store onions and garlic in your pantry, so buying in bulk to keep the cost down makes sense. Both go well in many dishes, including stir-fries, salads, soups, stews, and more.

8. Rice

Whole grains are positively encouraged in the Mediterranean Diet because they help protect your heart, improve digestion, and stabilize blood sugar. Those grains include barley, corn, oats, quinoa, bulgur, teff, and more, but these may not always be within your budget. Instead, try rice. It's much cheaper, and you can buy it anywhere. White rice is healthy, but brown rice is better, as it has more protein and fiber. You can eat rice on its own or add it to many dishes, including risotto, fish taco bowls, fried rice, and more.

9. Frozen Berries

Eating a wide variety of fruits and veggies is key to success on the Mediterranean Diet. The more different colors you can eat, the wider your nutrient intake, and berries offer plenty of fiber, minerals, antioxidants, vitamins, and anti-inflammatory properties. Eating a wide variety can also positively impact your brain health. However, berries aren't always in season, and fresh ones can go off quite quickly.

When you can't get fresh, use frozen. These are picked at their best and flash-frozen to keep their nutrients and flavor intact. Where fresh can only be stored in the fridge for a couple of days, frozen fruits can last for months in the freezer. They are less than half the cost and can be added to parfaits, smoothies, oats, yogurt, and even used in baking.

10. Oats

Oats are another staple; they are full of fiber and a budget-friendly way of getting your whole grains. Dried oats have a long shelf life and can be used to make energy balls, overnight oats, and more.

11. Frozen Greens

Leafy greens offer the most nutrients of virtually any vegetable, with one small serving packed with nutrients, vitamins, and minerals. However, unless you grow your own, they work out quite expensive. Buying fresh greens in bulk is no good unless you can use them all quickly, but frozen ones provide much better value for money. Although you can't use them in salads, you can use them in any recipes that call for greens to be cooked, such as casseroles, stews, soups, and stir-fries.

12. Corn

Corn is a whole grain and one of the main sources in many countries. It is also one of the cheaper grains and can be used fresh, frozen, or even canned, so long as it has no added sodium or sugar. Corn is full of vitamins, fiber, and antioxidants that help your overall health. Corn is also versatile and can be eaten grilled on the cob, raw or cooked in salads, tortillas, soups, stews, and more.

CHAPTER 12

7-DAY QUICK START MEAL PLAN

The Mediterranean Diet is easy enough to follow, but sometimes, you need a helping hand. The 7-day quick-start meal plan below is designed to be easy to follow.

Meal Prepping for the Week

First, you'll notice that some recipes are included more than once, so prepping ahead is a sure-fire way to help you stick to the diet:

1. Make the feta and pepper omelet muffins for the first day and freeze the rest. That way, you'll have breakfast already prepared for the third, fifth, and seventh days – you just have to remember to get them out the night before.

2. When you prep the overnight berry muesli for breakfast on the fourth day, make enough for two servings. Half can be left in the fridge, ready for breakfast on day six.

3. After dinner on the fourth day, prep two servings of the veggie chopped power salad and dressing for lunch on the fifth and sixth days.

7-Day Meal Plan

This meal plan is based on consuming 1500-1600 calories per day:

DAY ONE

MEAL	RECIPE
Breakfast	1 serving of feta and pepper omelet muffins 1 whole-wheat English muffin
Morning Snack	1 medium banana 1 tablespoon of natural peanut butter
Lunch	1 serving of avocado tuna salad 1 slice of whole-wheat bread
Afternoon Snack	¼ cup of hummus 1 medium celery stalk ½ cup of red bell pepper slices
Dinner	1 serving of balsamic mushroom and spinach pasta

DAY TWO

MEAL	RECIPE
Breakfast	1 serving of lemon-blueberry yogurt toast 1 orange
Morning Snack	1 cup of fresh raspberries 3 tbsp of roasted, unsalted cashews
Lunch	1 serving of chicken and vegetable quesadilla
Afternoon Snack	1 large pear 1 ounce of low-fat cheddar cheese
Dinner	1 serving of chickpea dumplings in curried tomato sauce

TIP: Save half a serving of the chickpea dumpling dish for tomorrow's lunch.

DAY THREE

MEAL	RECIPE
Breakfast	1 serving of feta and pepper omelet muffins 1 cup of blueberries
Morning Snack	1 serving of fig and honey yogurt
Lunch	½ a serving of chickpea dumplings in curried tomato sauce ½ whole wheat naan or pita
Afternoon Snack	1 plum 10 raw almonds
Dinner	1 serving of salmon rice bowl

DAY FOUR

MEAL	RECIPE
Breakfast	1 serving of overnight berry muesli
Morning Snack	1 medium apple ¾ cup of 1% cottage cheese
Lunch	Lentil salad with feta, tomatoes, cucumbers, and olives
Afternoon Snack	2 servings of lemon-parm popcorn
Dinner	1 serving of vegetable bowl with chicken and lemon tahini dressing

DAY FIVE

MEAL	RECIPE
Breakfast	1 serving of feta and pepper omelet muffins 1 whole-wheat English muffin
Morning Snack	2 clementines 1 ounce of low-fat cheddar 10 roasted, unsalted almonds
Lunch	1 serving of vegetarian power salad with creamy dressing
Afternoon Snack	1 serving of avocado pesto ½ cup of sliced carrots ½ cup of sliced cucumber
Dinner	1 serving of Southwestern cauliflower rice bowl with shrimp and avocado crema

DAY SIX

MEAL	RECIPE
Breakfast	1 serving of overnight berry muesli
Morning Snack	1 large pear ¼ cup of dry-roasted, unsalted, shelled pistachios
Lunch	1 serving of vegetarian power salad with creamy dressing
Afternoon Snack	½ cup of low-fat, plain Greek yogurt 1 tsp of organic honey ½ cup of pineapple
Dinner	1 serving of Dijon salmon and green bean pilaf

DAY SEVEN

MEAL	RECIPE
Breakfast	1 serving of feta and pepper omelet muffins 1 whole-wheat English muffin
Morning Snack	1 medium banana 1 tbsp of natural peanut butter
Lunch	1 serving of Green Goddess chickpea salad
Afternoon Snack	1 serving of cinnamon popcorn
Dinner	1 serving of chicken parmesan and quinoa stuffed peppers

Hope you enjoyed that 7-day meal plan

As an exclusive offer, I created a **7-Day Quick Start Grocery Checklist** that makes buying the items for above easier.

You can access your copy here:
https://empirepublishingso.wixsite.com/mediterranean-diet-1

Efficient Meal Preparation

If you have a busy lifestyle, are constantly working on a tight schedule, and struggle to find time to prepare healthy meals, you are not alone. That's where meal prepping comes in, allowing you to use what time you do have available to prep ahead for busier days.

1. **Plan Your Meals Each Week:** Once a week, sit down and plan your meals for the week ahead. Then, draw up your shopping list so that when you do your shopping, you are organized and not tempted to buy what you don't need.

2. **Pick Easy Recipes:** Choose recipes that won't take much preparation time or complicated ingredients and instructions. Grain bowls, salads, grilled fish, or chicken and veggies are all healthy, fulfilling meals that are easy and quick to make.

3. **Batch-Prep:** Set time aside on a day off to prep in batches. This doesn't just apply to complete meals. You can also prep your ingredients for the week ahead – wash and cut up fruit and vegetables, cook grains, marinate proteins, etc.

4. **Use Pre-Cut or Frozen Veggies and Fruits:** There is nothing wrong with purchasing pre-cut foods or frozen versions.

5. **Use Canned Foods:** Canned beans, tomatoes, salmon, tuna, etc., are all fine to us and make prepping even quicker and easier. Make sure they don't have added sugar, salt, or preservatives.

6. **Keep Healthy Staples to Hand:** This includes extra virgin olive oil, herbs, spices, grains, etc., so you have everything you need for prepping.

7. **Prep Versatile Ingredients:** Spend some time roasting veggies, grilling fish and chicken, cooking grains, and storing them so you can use them as needed during the week.

8. **Make Salads in Mason Jars:** Prepare a range of different Mason Jar salads and refrigerate them so you can grab them and go during the week. Layer your healthy ingredients, then give them a quick shake before eating.

9. **Use Food Prep Containers:** These will help you prep the right size portions and help you avoid overeating.

10. **Freeze the Extras:** When you make a dish, make extra and freeze the rest for meals further down the line when you haven't got the time to make it from scratch.

11. **Stock Up on Healthy Snacks:** Have plenty of nuts, seeds, fresh fruit, and yogurt on hand, so you don't need to spend time prepping your snacks.

12. **Use an Instant Pot or Slow Cooker:** Especially when making soups, stews, or one-pot recipes, as these save you a whole lot of time. Simply spend a few minutes prepping in the morning, chuck it all in a slow cooker, and leave it cooking for the day – dinner is served when you get home from work.

Don't forget that the Mediterranean Diet revolves around fresh, whole, unprocessed foods, so even if you are short on time, you should still try to include as much fresh fruit, veggies, and whole grains in your diet.

Top Tips for Storing and Heating Prepped Meals

When you prep your meals, you can make enough food for the next few days or weeks without breaking too much of a sweat. However, it doesn't matter how much you prep ahead. It's all a waste of time if you don't store your meals properly, and if you don't reheat them properly, they'll taste awful and lose much of their goodness.

In the Refrigerator:

- **Use Airtight Containers:** And make sure they are sealed properly. These can slow bacterial growth and keep your food fresher longer. Glass jars are great for soups, while plastic is ideal for rice and proteins. Salad dressings and small salads can easily be stored in Mason jars.
- **Use Paper Towels to Store Diced Fruit and Veggies:** When you prep your fruits and veggies, put paper towels into the storage container to help keep the food dry. This will help them last longer.

- **Refrigerate at Lower Than 40°F (4°C):** The ideal temperature is 35 to 38°F as bacteria will thrive above 40°F, leading to quick spoilage.

- **Don't Store Leftovers in the Fridge Door:** That is the one part of your fridge most vulnerable to temperature changes when the door is opened. Also, be aware that the bottom of the fridge is the coldest place, so store prepped food on the bottom shelf, not the top. The top shelf is better for eggs and other foods with a longer shelf life.

- **Don't Leave Leftover Meat Too Long:** Even when stored in the fridge, seafood, poultry, and red meat will only last for up to five days, so make sure you consume them before then. Make sure you understand this for prepped meals containing these ingredients.

- **Store Your Produce Whole:** Whole veggies and fruits have a longer shelf life, lasting up to two weeks or even longer when stored properly. Cut-up fruits and veggies will normally only last a day or two.

- **Don't Store Hot Food:** Always let cooked food cool for 30 minutes before refrigerating it. This stops condensation from making the food soggy. That said, ensure you refrigerate them before they reach room temperature to avoid bacterial growth.

- **Choose Long-Lasting Ingredients:** Good meal prep depends on using the right ingredients. Meals made with cheese, pasta, and grains are better for refrigerator storage than berries, avocados, and other perishable ingredients.

- **Don't Overload Your Fridge:** This prevents the cold air from circulating and causes temperature fluctuations that can warm food up to a temperature where bacteria grows and spoils the food.

In the Freezer:

- **Keep the Freezer at 0°F (-18°C):** This ensures the best conditions for food storage. If the temperature is too high or the food doesn't freeze properly, it can lead to spoilage.
- **Only Freeze the Right Ingredients:** Some foods will change taste and texture when they freeze and won't be so nice. Meals containing fish, poultry, beef, and cut veggies/fruits tend to be better when thawed, especially if you use them in stews and soups.
- **Store Food in Plastic Containers:** Resealable bags will work, too, so long as they are sturdy and food-grade. Glass will expand when it freezes and can crack, so only use glass containers if they are certified to withstand subzero temperatures.
- **Thaw Your Food in the Refrigerator:** Thawing food at room temperature can result in bacterial growth. When you thaw food in the refrigerator, that growth is slowed enough for the food to be safe the following day.
- **Cut Out the Freezer Burn:** When food meets moisture in the freezer, it can cause freezer burn. Cut off any that you see to ensure your meals are enjoyable. Of course, you could avoid it in the first place by ensuring your food is suitably contained.

- **Let Your Food Cool Before You Freeze It:** You should always allow food to cool down to room temperature to remove the risk of moisture in the storage container. Also, when you place warm foods in the freezer, the temperature can rise in other foods, leading to bacterial growth and spoilage.

- **Freeze in Portions:** When you freeze food in large blocks, the whole lot has to be defrosted. Instead, split your food into portions first, then you only have to remove what you need. Plus, some foods cannot be refrozen, and others lose quality and taste.

Reheating Prepped Food

Just as important as how you store food is how you reheat it:

- **Use Glass Dishes to Microwave Prepped Meals:** If you store your meal in a glass container, put the whole thing in the microwave. However, you cannot put it in an oven as it could shatter when the hot glass meets the cooler air of your kitchen.

- **Use Plates to Reheat Meals Stored in Plastic Containers:** When you use plastic bags or containers to store food, transfer it to a plate before microwaving it. Heated plastic can cause chemicals to leach out into your food, putting your health at risk.

- **Using the Oven:** If you prefer to use an oven, put parchment paper on a baking sheet and place your meal on it. This ensures the heat is distributed evenly through the food and stops it from going soggy.

- **Get the Temperature Right:** Reheated food should have an internal temperature of about 165°F (74°C) before you eat it. That temperature will kill off any bacteria that may have formed in the food, making it safe to eat.

- **Consider Your Portion Sizes:** When you reheat food, only reheat it for as long as the portion size needs. The larger the meal, the longer the time to make sure it gets hot through.

- **Undercook Some Things Before Storing Them:** If you are making meals purely for storage, undercook beef, shrimp, and other similar ingredients a little. That way, when you reheat the food, it won't go soggy or be overcooked, and it will have a better flavor.

- **Use Water if Reheating on Your Stove:** If you transfer food to a saucepan to reheat on the stove, add a little water occasionally to help keep the moisture in the food and keep the textures and flavor good.

- **Reheat in Date Order:** Always label your food with the date you made it and put newer meals at the back. That way, you eat the older food first, reducing the risk of spoilage.

Bringing The Mediterranean to Your Cooking

One of the easiest ways of transitioning to the Mediterranean Diet is gradually introducing Mediterranean elements to your cooking and meal prep. These simple tips will help you do just that:

Start with a Mediterranean breakfast:

Breakfast is an easy meal to start with, as you can easily add some Mediterranean flavor to help boost your daily nutrition. Here are some ideas to help you:

- Add fruits, like diced peaches or figs, to your yogurt, oatmeal, or toast.
- Go for whole-grain cereals and breads.
- Have avocado toast with a little olive oil drizzled over, or blend some olive oil into your smoothie.

Here's an easy recipe to make to kickstart your day. The yogurt provides probiotics, the berries are full of antioxidants, and the granola gives you crunch and fiber:

Strawberry-Yogurt Parfait

Ingredients:

- 1 ½ cups of full-fat, plain Greek yogurt
- 1 cup of halved fresh strawberries
- ½ cup of healthy muesli
- 2 tsp of organic honey
- 1 tsp of vanilla extract

Instructions:

1. Mix the yogurt and vanilla together.

2. Divide the yogurt between two bowls, top with strawberries and muesli, and finish with a honey drizzle. Serve straight away.

NOTE

If you don't intend to eat it immediately, don't add the muesli until just before serving.

Have a Mediterranean lunch:

Eating the right meal at lunchtime can give your body the fuel it needs to keep going through the afternoon, and the best way to do that is with a Mediterranean-style lunch, like these easy-to-prepare dishes:

- Greek salad with cucumber, tomato, feta cheese, olives, and olive oil.

- Sandwich on whole-grain bread with grilled turkey or chicken breast, tomatoes, lettuce, and tzatziki sauce as a spread.

- A grain bowl with quinoa, cucumber, diced pepper, chickpeas, cherry tomatoes, and lemon vinaigrette.

Try this salad, the perfect combination of fresh veggies, whole grains, and that all-important olive oil:

Mediterranean Quinoa Salad

Serves: 4

Ingredients:

- 1 cup of dry quinoa
- 2 cups of water
- 1 diced yellow or red bell pepper
- ½ - 1 cup of diced cucumber
- ½ - 1 cup of halved cherry tomatoes
- ½ cup of green or black olives
- ½ red onion, diced
- ½ cup of crumbled feta cheese
- ¼ cup of fresh cilantro leaves

Instructions:

- Bring the water to a boil and add the quinoa. Put the lid on, reduce the heat, and simmer for about 10 to 15 minutes – all the water should be absorbed.

- Take the lid off, use a fork to fluff the quinoa, and put it in a bowl.

- Add all the other ingredients, toss, and serve with a generous drizzle of olive oil.

- You can let the quinoa cool down first if you prefer, and if you follow a dairy-free diet, simply leave the cheese out.

Have Mediterranean-style snacks to hand

Healthy snacks are a big part of Mediterranean eating, designed to provide you with plenty of nutrition while stopping you from eating too much at your main meals. Here are some ideas:

- Roasted chickpeas are easy to make and full of fiber and protein.

- Cucumber with tzatziki makes a refreshing snack, the crisp cucumber contrasting with the creamy yogurt dip.

- Dried fruits and nuts are perfect for a quick boost of energy and are full of natural sweetness and healthy fat.

Try this recipe for a quick, easy, healthy snack:

Spiced Nuts

Ingredients:

- 3 cups of raw nuts – a mixture of walnuts, almonds, cashews, etc.

- 1 12 tbsp of extra virgin olive oil

- ½ tsp of coarse Himalayan pink salt

- ½ tsp of chili powder

- ½ tsp of cumin

- ½ tsp of chili powder

- ¼ tsp of cayenne

- ¼ tsp of garlic granules

- 1/8 tsp of pepper

Instructions:

- Preheat your oven to 350°F and put parchment paper on a baking sheet.

- Put the nuts in a bowl and add the spices and olive oil. Toss to coat all the nuts.

- Place the nuts in one layer on the sheet and bake for about 15 minutes. Remove them from the oven, let them cool completely, and put them in an airtight container until you want them.

Have a Mediterranean Dinner

Mediterranean-style dinners require a focus on heart-healthy, delicious foods:

- **Seafood:** This is one of the main protein sources in the Mediterranean, containing plenty of heart and brain-healthy omega-3 fatty acids.

- **Vegetables:** Eat a good variety of different-colored veggies to get a wide range of nutrients.

- **Herbs:** These are healthier and tastier ways to flavor food without using salt.

Try the following recipe, an excellent combination of these three principles:

Greek Shrimp and Feta Skillet

Serves: 4

Ingredients:

- 1 lb. of cooked, deveined shrimp, tails removed

- 6 ounces of crumbled feta

- 1 diced yellow onion

- 2 tbsp of extra virgin olive oil

- 3 minced garlic cloves

- 1 can of drained diced tomatoes (28 ounces)

- 1 ½ tsp of dried oregano

- 1 ½ tsp of dried parsley

- ½ tsp of red pepper flakes

- Salt and pepper for seasoning

- Fresh basil for garnish

Instructions:

- Heat the oil in a skillet over medium heat. Cook the onion and garlic until the onions are soft.

- Add the tomatoes, dried herbs, pepper flakes, and season with salt and pepper. Stir and let it come to a simmer.

- Add the shrimp and let them warm up.

- Once the shrimp are warm, turn the heat off and sprinkle with the feta cheese. Let it melt and serve hot.

Use healthy fats for dressing and cooking:

The obvious one is olive oil, the healthiest of all fats. It is full of healthy monounsaturated fats that help balance cholesterol, protect the heart, and boost overall well-being. Here are some easy ways to use olive oil:

- Sauté your veggies

- Use it in dressings
- Drizzle it over whole-grain bread

Other healthy fats include avocado oil, coconut oil, coconut milk, seeds, and nuts, all excellent sources of monounsaturated fats, minerals, and vitamins.

Have fresh fruits and colorful veggies:

Vegetables and fruits are a big part of the Mediterranean lifestyle, especially seasonal ones that offer the best nutrients and flavors:

- **Salads:** Leafy greens, crisp cucumbers, juicy tomatoes, and sweet, crunchy bell peppers combine into a wonderfully tasty, light meal.
- **Smoothies:** Kale or spinach and berries with Greek yogurt make a quick, flavorful, healthy snack.
- **Roast Veggies:** Roasting veggies with herbs and olive oil brings out their flavors and sweetness.

Try whole-grain alternatives:

Perhaps one of the biggest ways to enter the Mediterranean lifestyle is to eat whole-grain instead of refined-grain foods. That means adding some of the following to your diet:

- **Quinoa:** high in protein and a good base for sides and salads.
- **Barley:** perfect for stews and soups.
- **Farro:** great for stir-fries and pilafs.

Ditch refined grains for whole grains wherever possible, i.e., swapping white bread for whole-grain, white pasta and rice for brown alternatives, or using the grains above instead of rice.

Eat moderate amounts of poultry and fish:

Seafood and lean poultry are healthy protein sources without adding the saturated fat that red meat provides. Lean proteins are important because they help your overall health and help you maintain your muscles. Fatty fish is an excellent protein source, providing heart-healthy fats and other nutrients that support the brain.

Here's a great recipe combining all these principles:

Grilled Lemon-Herb Chicken Breast

Ingredients:

- 4 skinless, boneless chicken breasts
- 2 tbsp of extra virgin olive oil
- 1 tbsp of chopped herbs – rosemary, basil, thyme, etc.
- Juice and zest from a lemon
- Salt and pepper for seasoning

Instructions:

1. Preheat the grill to medium-high.
2. Mix the juice, zest, oil, and herbs and season to taste.
3. Lay the breasts on the hot grill, brush the herbed oil over them, and cook on both sides for six to eight minutes. When cooked, a meat thermometer inserted in the thickest part should read 165°F.
4. Serve with a crisp salad or steamed fresh veggies.

Lean chicken and turkey are the easy choices, but what about seafood? Some of the best choices are fatty fishes high in omega-s, like tuna, salmon, and mackerel, and there are three healthy ways to prepare them:

- **Grill:** Marinate or brush them with spics and herbs for an amazing flavor.

- **Baake:** Drizzle with a little olive oil and season to your taste.

- **Sauté:** Cook them lightly with a small amount of olive oil until flaky and tender.

Get healthy fats and proteins from nuts and legumes:

Nuts and legumes are an important part of the Mediterranean Diet as they are packed with nutrition, including plant proteins and healthy fasts. Some easy ways to include them are:

- **Stews and Soups:** Add chickpeas, lentils, or beans to make nutritious, filling stews and soups.

- **Trail Mix:** Make your own trail mix with a combination of nuts, seeds, and dried fruits for a boost of energy.

- **Salad Toppings:** Sprinkle cooked legumes or a handful of nuts on top of a salad for a healthy dose of nutrients.

Try this hearty, nutritional soup:

Instant Pot Lentil and Vegetable Soup

Ingredients:

- 2 cans of diced tomatoes (14 ½ ounces each)

- 4 cups of chicken bone broth

- 1 diced yellow onion

- 2 cups of diced carrots

- 2 cups of diced celery

- 1 ½ cups of dried lentils – any color or mixture

- 1 tbsp of minced garlic

- 1 tsp of pink Himalayan salt

- 1 tsp of smoked paprika

- 1 tsp of dried thyme

- ½ tsp of black pepper

Instructions:

1. Place everything in your Instant Pot and stir well.

2. Put the lid on and pressure cook for 20 minutes on HIGH. Release the pressure gradually once cooked.

3. Stir and serve.

Integrating the Mediterranean Diet into your lifestyle is as simple as following the above tips. Learn to eat mindfully, share your meals with friends and family, and enjoy every mouthful of delicious food, knowing it benefits your health in many ways.

CONCLUSION

PUTTING IT ALL TOGETHER

You've reached the end of this guide, and hopefully, you've enjoyed the journey. As you have learned, the Mediterranean Diet is less of a diet and more of a lifestyle. It's about more than what you eat. It's about your mindset, being active, and socializing over meal times.

This guide has been your one-stop-shop for following this lifestyle, and you learned what the diet is all about, how to follow it, how to customize it to your requirements, and the benefits of using seasonal ingredients.

You also learned about its amazing health benefits. What other diet can help you reduce your risks of chronic diseases, help you maintain a healthy weight, and provide all the nutrition your body needs for optimal functioning without being restrictive? None. The Mediterranean Diet is the only one that does all that and more. Perhaps more important, though, is learning to adopt the Mediterranean mindset. That means incorporating activity into your daily life, be it a walk around the park or a two-hour gym session. It means making your meals a social event, practicing mindful eating, learning to embrace olive oil, using local and seasonal ingredients, learning to love nature, and focusing on keeping your happiness and mental health in tip-top condition.

You then learned what foods you can and should include in your diet, what you should limit or eliminate altogether, and the health benefits of each type of food before being introduced to some of the healthiest recipes, full of flavor and nutrition, that you can eat. You got a sample 7-day plan and an idea of what to put on your grocery list. You learned efficient meal prep, how to store and reheat your prepped meals, and how to bring the Mediterranean to your everyday cooking.

Herbs and spices are an important part of the Mediterranean Diet, and you learned about the popular ones to use and keep in your pantry. You learned how to make your own seasonings and grow herbs at home. You also learned some of the essential techniques used in Mediterranean cooking and how to incorporate them into your own meal prep.

Lastly, you learned how to follow the Mediterranean Diet on a budget. It might seem at first glance that this diet is only for those with deep pockets, but it is actually one of the cheaper ones. There are plenty of budget-friendly sources of whole grains and proteins, and frozen, dried, and canned foods are encouraged where you can't get fresh foods.

The Mediterranean Diet is undoubtedly one of the easiest to follow, and it is easy to adapt it to your own preferences, lifestyle choices, or dietary requirements. There are no hard and fast rules or set diet plans to follow, and you are encouraged to put your own personal touch on things and follow the plan in a way you will stick to.

Embrace the Mediterranean way of life, enjoy their delicious cuisine, and benefit from all the wonderful health benefits. This is one diet that, once you start following it, you'll continue. The fact that it isn't restrictive makes it so much easier to follow, and you can ease your way into it by making simple food swaps, upping your activity level, and learning to get social.

REFERENCES

9 Mediterranean Lifestyle Habits That Are Just As Important As Diet. (2023, April 18). FitOn - #1 Free Fitness App, Stop Paying for Home Workouts. https://fitonapp.com/wellness/mediterranean-lifestyle-habits/

10 Ways to Incorporate the Mediterranean Diet Into Your Daily Routine. (n.d.). Beyond the Brambleberry. https://www.beyondthebrambleberry.com/blog/incorporate-mediterranean-diet-into-daily-routine

25 Expert Advice on Storing Meal Prep Food for Longer Freshness. (n.d.). Www.mealvillage.com. https://www.mealvillage.com/blog/store-meal-prep-food-tips.jsp

Better Health Channel. (2022, September 12). *Fruit and vegetables.* Vic.gov.au. https://www.betterhealth.vic.gov.au/health/HealthyLiving/fruit-and-vegetables

Boston, 677 H. A., & Ma 02115 +1495-1000. (2018, January 16). *Diet Review: Mediterranean Diet.* The Nutrition Source. https://www.hsph.harvard.edu/nutritionsource/healthy-weight/diet-reviews/mediterranean-diet/

Dec 10, F. | H. 4020 | R., & Print, 2020 |. (n.d.). *Go Lean With Protein.* Home & Garden Information Center | Clemson University, South Carolina. https://hgic.clemson.edu/factsheet/go-lean-with-protein/

Drop Bio Health | 12 principles of the Mediterranean diet. (n.d.). Www.dropbiohealth.com. https://www.dropbiohealth.com/health-resources/mediterranean-diet

Essential Techniques for Authentic Mediterranean Cooking. (n.d.). Rana's Recipe. https://ranasrecipe.com/recipe_info/essential-techniques-for-authentic-mediterranean-cooking/

FARRINGTON'S. (2020, February 3). *WHY SHOULD I EAT SEASONAL FOOD?* FARRINGTON'S | Farm Shop, Café, Soft Play & Much More. https://www.farringtons.co.uk/post/eat-the-seasons-seasonal-local-fruit-and-vegetables-from-farrington-s-farm-in-bristol

Feb. 24, N. M., & 2024. (2019, January 29). *20 Mediterranean Spices and Herbs.* Taste of Home. https://www.tasteofhome.com/article/mediterranean-diet-herbs/

Fullenweider, P., MS, & RD. (2023, September 11). *10 Vegan Mediterranean Recipes with 10g+ of Protein - Fully Mediterranean.* https://fullymediterranean.com/featured/vegan-mediterranean-recipes/

Fully Mediterranean - Mediterranean Diet Recipes & Counseling. (2017, May 26). https://fullymediterranean.com/

Harvard Health Publishing. (2016, January 16). *8 steps to mindful eating.* Harvard Health; Harvard Health. https://www.health.harvard.edu/staying-healthy/8-steps-to-mindful-eating

Healthy Recipes, Healthy Eating. (2019). EatingWell. https://www.eatingwell.com/

How To Grow Herbs At Home: 9 Herbs You Can Easily Grow Indoors. (2023, December 22). AllThatGrows. https://www.allthatgrows.in/blogs/posts/how-to-grow-herbs-at-home

How to Meal Prep for the Mediterranean Diet for Beginners. (n.d.). Beyond the Brambleberry. https://www.beyondthebrambleberry.com/blog/meal-prep-mediterranean-diet

How To Start The Mediterranean Diet - Fully Mediterranean. (2023, January 10). https://fullymediterranean.com/featured/how-to-start-the-mediterranean-diet/

Lamb, J. (2020, May 2). *The Essential Guide to Reheating Meal Prepped Food.* A Dash of Macros. https://adashofmacros.com/reheating-meal-prepped-food/

Living, M. (2023, January 3). *Mediterranean Diet Grocery and Shopping List.* Mediterranean Living. https://www.mediterraneanliving.com/mediterranean-diet-grocery-and-shopping-list/#extra-virgin-olive-oil

Mayo Clinic. (2022, December 10). *The whole truth about whole grains.* Mayo Clinic. https://www.mayoclinic.org/healthy-lifestyle/nutrition-and-healthy-eating/in-depth/whole-grains/art-20047826

McManus, K. (2019, March 11). *A practical guide to the Mediterranean diet.* Harvard Health Blog. https://www.health.harvard.edu/blog/a-practical-guide-to-the-mediterranean-diet-2019032116194

Mediterranean Diet 101: Meal Plan, Foods List, and Tips. (2021, September 17). Healthline. https://www.healthline.com/nutrition/mediterranean-diet-meal-plan#faq

Mediterranean Diet and Olive Oil. (n.d.). Olive Oils from Spain. https://www.oliveoilsfromspain.org/olive-oil-news/what-mediterranean-diet/

Mediterranean Diet: 8 Scientific Benefits, According to New Research. (2023, April 25). Healthline. https://www.healthline.com/health-news/8-ways-the-mediterranean-diet-can-help-you-live-a-longer-and-healthier-life#How-to-start-the-Mediterranean-diet

Mediterranean Diet: Benefits, Food List And Meal Plans. (2024, January 9). Forbes Health. https://www.forbes.com/health/nutrition/diet/what-is-the-mediterranean-diet/

Mediterreanean Recipes, Diet & Lifestyle | The Mediterranean Dish. (2019, October 29). The Mediterranean Dish. https://www.themediterraneandish.com/

Paravantes, E. (2016, March 30). *6 Mediterranean Food Swaps That Will Instantly Make Your Diet Healthier.* https://www.olivetomato.com/6-mediterranean-food-swaps-that-will-instantly-make-your-diet-healthier/

Paravantes, E. (2021, January 12). *The Mediterranean Diet on a Budget: 12 Tips That Will Save you Money -.* https://www.olivetomato.com/the-mediterranean-diet-on-a-budget-12-tips-that-will-save-you-money/

Picard, C. (2019). *Recipe Ideas, Product Reviews, Home Decor Inspiration, and Beauty Tips - Good Housekeeping.* Good Housekeeping; Good Housekeeping. https://www.goodhousekeeping.com/

The 12 Best Mediterranean Diet Foods on a Budget, According to a Dietitian. (n.d.). EatingWell. https://www.eatingwell.com/article/8059181/best-budget-friendly-mediterranean-diet-foods/

Tognon, G. (2018, July 10). *The history of the Mediterranean diet.* Gianluca Tognon. https://www.gianlucatognon.com/history-mediterranean-diet/

Traditional Med Diet. (n.d.). Oldways. https://oldwayspt.org/traditional-diets/mediterranean-diet/traditional-med-diet

Zelman, K. M., MPH, RD, & LD. (n.d.). *Sweets and Treats in a Healthy Diet.* WebMD. https://www.webmd.com/diet/features/sweets-treats-healthy-diet

Made in United States
Troutdale, OR
11/02/2024